BILLY GRAHAM

Evangelistic Association

Always Good News.

Dear Friend,

I am pleased to send you this copy of *Faith is For Weak People* by Ray Comfort. Ray is an apologist, best-selling author, and the founder and CEO of Living Waters Ministry. He also co-hosts the award-winning TV program *The Way of the Master*.

In God's Word, He tells believers to "*always be prepared to give an answer to everyone who asks you to give the reason for the hope that you have*" (1 Pctcr 3:15, NIV). In *Faith is For Weak People*, Ray helps prepare you to do just that. This powerful book contains Scriptural responses to common objections to Christianity—and Biblical insight to help you answer those questions with the love of Jesus Christ. It's my prayer that this book will strengthen your own faith and give you practical ways to share it with others.

If your life has been touched in a special way through the ministries of the Billy Graham Evangelistic Association (BGEA), we would love to hear from you. Testimonies to the power of God impact others in countless ways. The psalmist declared: "*Come and see the works of God; He is awesome in His doing toward the sons of men*" (Psalm 66:5, NKJV).

I'm so thankful for how God has worked through BGEA for 70 years, and I'm excited about what He will do in the years ahead as the Gospel of Jesus Christ is proclaimed around the world. May He richly bless you.

Sincerely,

Franklin Graham
President

If you would like to know more about our ministry, please contact us:

IN THE U.S.:
Billy Graham Evangelistic Association
1 Billy Graham Parkway
Charlotte, NC 28201-0001
BillyGraham.org
info@bgea.org
Toll-free: 1-877-247-2426

IN CANADA:
Billy Graham Evangelistic
    Association of Canada
20 Hopewell Way NE
Calgary, AB T3J 5H5
BillyGraham.ca
Toll-free: 1-888-393-0003

FAITH IS FOR
WEAK
PEOPLE

FAITH IS FOR
WEAK
PEOPLE

**Responding to the
Top 20 Objections
to the Gospel**

RAY COMFORT

BakerBooks

a division of Baker Publishing Group
Grand Rapids, Michigan

This *Billy Graham Library Selection* special edition is published with
permission from Baker Books, a division of Baker Publishing Group.

©2019 by Ray Comfort

Published by Baker Books
a division of Baker Publishing Group
PO Box 6287, Grand Rapids, MI 49516-6287
www.bakerbooks.com

Printed in the United States of America

Library of Congress Cataloging-in-Publication Data
Names: Comfort, Ray, author.
Title: Faith is for weak people: responding to the top 20 objections to the Gospel / Ray Comfort.
Description: Grand Rapids: Baker Publishing Group, 2019. | Includes
    bibliographical references.
Identifiers: LCCN 2018045154 | ISBN 9780801093982 (pbk.)
Subjects: LCSH: Apologetics—Miscellanea.
Classification: LCC BT1103 .C644 2019 | DDC 239—dc23
LC record available at https://lccn.loc.gov/2018045154
ISBN 978-1-59328-647-7 (BGEA edition)

19 20 21 22 23 24 25   7 6 5 4 3 2 1

To all those who don't believe
but who are prepared to go
where the evidence leads.

Contents

Introduction

My car's gas gauge was very close to "E." Of course, the E stands for "Enough," but the time had come when I needed to put gas in the tank. I wasn't being one of those last-minute-always-late people. I wanted the tank to get low so that it would take thirty dollars' worth and reach the "F" ("Finished").

As I pulled into the gas station, I saw that two thoughtless drivers had positioned their cars so that I would be forced to park with our cars facing each other. That meant that when the person had finished, he would have to back out to get out. So I decided I would drive around the closest car and maneuver until I had my gas tank on the right side of the pump.

It didn't go as planned. Another car pulled into the station and unwittingly blocked me. After him, a police officer drove in. He made me feel a little nervous. Suddenly I was going back and forth with a police officer in close proximity. It was like one of those viral videos. I felt sure the security camera would be given to the TV nightly news. I would provide the evening's comic relief after all the depressing news.

After what felt like days, I had positioned the car correctly, locked it, had not been arrested, and was inside the station purchasing thirty dollars' worth of gas for my VW Beetle. The man behind the thick glass asked me in a thick accent whether I wanted debit or credit for my card. I responded and then slid it through the machine. Nothing happened. I tried again. The card declined, which was embarrassing. But all was well. I had another in my wallet. I put that in and it declined also. This was because it was a Home Depot card, which I didn't realize only worked in Home Depot.

Mr. Thick Accent suddenly became very impatient with me. His impatience turned into anger. This wasn't supposed to be happening. I was the customer, and the customer is always right, even if he's an idiot and can't position his car or use a credit card.

I consoled myself with the thought that the man must have been having a bad day. He was stuck behind glass like a goldfish, asking people all day whether their purchase was debit or credit. I decided to show him a little kindness. I always carry gift cards to give to people after I share the gospel. They are only five-dollar cards, but they are evident tokens of love and can speak louder than the most eloquent sermon. I got out a Subway card and kindly slid it through the slot under the thick glass partition, hoping it would turn away wrath.

I said, "Here's a gift for you." *This would calm him down,* I thought. It never fails.

It made him worse. He thought I was giving him another credit card and telling him to put it through the slot. It just added fuel to the fire, and he flared up and tossed it back at me. This was a simple misunderstanding that would resolve itself in seconds, so I tossed it back at him as if we were playing tennis.

He volleyed back, "What am I going to do with this? It's a Subway card!"

I hit back, "This is a gift card for you. I saw that you were having a tough day and want to make your life happier. It's a free lunch for you."

Fifteen love.

His eyes widened as he began to see that it was a misunderstanding, but he covered his embarrassment by angrily pushing it back under the glass, saying that he didn't want it. I quickly exited the station, returned later with cash, and was treated kindly by a new attendant.

As Christians, we are not only separate from this world, but we speak a different language. All we want is to give them the ultimate free lunch: "The gift of God is eternal life through Jesus Christ our Lord" (Rom. 6:23 KJV). But there are things that get lost in translation. Some think we're intellectually bankrupt or we are after their money or we want them to join some weird cult. They also don't like the fact that the lunch comes through "Jesus Christ our Lord." His name makes demons tremble and sinners nervous.

But John the Baptist said:

> Prepare the way of the Lord;
> Make His paths straight.
> Every valley should be filled
> And every mountain and hill brought low;
> The crooked places shall be made straight

And the rough ways smooth;
And all flesh shall see the salvation of God.
    (Luke 3:4–6).

In other words, the matter of eternal salvation is so important that every stumbling block to the Savior and every misunderstanding should be removed.

That's what this book is about. We love the lost and don't want anything to hinder a dying world from coming to Jesus Christ. Some have mountains of greed or bitterness or pride or legitimate questions. For others, there is a great valley between them and God. They are going through the depths of suffering, pain, or disease and are trapped in the valley of the shadow of death. They live in the quiet despair of hopelessness.

With the help of God, we can bring the mountains low and fill up the valleys. Fortunately, there is an effective and biblical way to humble the proud, awaken the complacent, and bring a living hope to the humble. God hasn't left us helpless in these most important issues. It just takes a little maneuvering.

May He use this book to fill your tank to the full.

Ray Comfort

Big Things First—Dealing with the Goliath of Fear

S tatistics tell us that not too many Christians share their faith.[1]

They are busy letting their light shine in other legitimate areas of life. But when we direct our efforts specifically toward issues such as racism, sexual perversion, greed, hatred, rape, adultery, anger, violence, poverty, gangs, corruption, pedophilia, alcoholism, pornography, drug abuse, fornication, abortion, and more, we must keep in mind that we are merely fighting the symptoms of the disease of sin. The gospel is the ultimate cure—and the only cure—to all.

You are reading a book on the subject of apologetics, so I'm sure you know this truth about the gospel and want to be effective in sharing the gospel cure. I also trust you've had the sobering realization that our agendas are overshadowed by something much more concerning than all these social issues combined—the existence of hell. Someone may be a racist, and we may want him to be lovingly accepting of all races, but the gospel wasn't given to be a cure for racism. The same thought applies to the adulterer or the alcoholic. Faithfulness in marriage and living a sober lifestyle aren't the chief goal of the gospel. They are the fruit of it. The goal is to see people saved from the just wrath of a holy God by being clothed with the righteousness of Jesus Christ. If we lose sight of this goal, we reduce the church to a social club of well-meaning do-gooders. And the world is full of them—from skilled marriage and drug counselors to the many worthy secular service organizations. They all strive to make lives happier, and they often achieve that goal.

To be effective we must know our goal—sharing the gospel. We must also know what to say when it comes to suffering, the existence of God, and the many other questions that arise when we involve ourselves in what Charles Spurgeon rightly called the "irksome" task of evangelism.[2]

But knowing our goal and knowing what to say are not enough if we are paralyzed by our fears. We are involved in a war, and having weapons in hand is not enough if soldiers are consumed with a fear that keeps them confined to the barracks. We will devote two entire chapters to addressing fear and revealing something in our arsenal that is far more important than the weapon of apologetics.

Forty-Five Years

For more than forty-five years, I have regularly shared the gospel with people from all walks of life. Yet I still battle fear. I fear the initial approach. I fear rejection. The battle that I continually have with fear is very real; fear is an enemy that shadows my every move. But I have found a light that dissipates the shadow.

Goliath is a household name even thousands of years after his death. As *Einstein* became a synonym for *genius*, *Goliath* became a synonym for *giant*.

The defeat of the bully is always a success at the box office. The nastier the bully is to some poor loser, the sweeter it is to see the loser win. Little David took on the big bully and instantly became a national hero and a historical icon for courage.

Experts disagree about Goliath's height. Some say he was six feet nine, while others say he was more than nine feet ten. I take the high road and go for the nine feet, because I doubt that the entire army of Israel would be terrified by someone who was only nine inches taller than the average soldier.

Let's pick up the story and look at how we can use this famous incident to deal with our personal taunting Goliath.

Then [David] took his staff in his hand; and he chose for himself five smooth stones from the brook, and put them in a shepherd's bag, in a pouch which he had, and his sling was in his hand. And he drew near to the Philistine. So the Philistine came, and began drawing near to David, and the man who bore the shield went before him. And when the Philistine looked about and saw David, he disdained him; for he was only a youth, ruddy and good-looking. So the Philistine said to David, "Am I a dog, that you come to me with sticks?" And the Philistine cursed David by his gods. And the Philistine said to David, "Come to me, and I will give your flesh to the birds of the air and the beasts of the field!" Then David said to the Philistine, "You come to me with a sword, with a spear, and with a javelin. But I come to you in the name of the LORD of hosts, the God of the armies of Israel, whom you have defied. This day the LORD will deliver you into my hand, and I will strike you and take your head from you. And this day I will give the carcasses of the camp of the Philistines to the birds of the air and the wild beasts of the earth, that all the earth may know that there is a God in Israel. Then all this assembly shall know that the LORD does not save with sword and spear; for the battle is the LORD's, and He will give you into our hands."

So it was, when the Philistine arose and came and drew near to meet David, that David hurried and ran toward the army to meet the Philistine. Then David put his hand in his bag and took out a stone; and he slung it and struck the Philistine in his forehead, so that the stone sank into his forehead, and he fell on his face to the earth. So David prevailed over the Philistine with a sling and a stone, and struck the Philistine and killed him. But there was no sword in the hand of David. Therefore David ran and stood over the Philistine, took his sword and drew it out of its sheath and killed him, and cut off his head with it." (1 Sam. 17:40–51)

There are two lessons here. The first one is obvious, and I'm sure you know it. But you may not be familiar with the second.

Here's the first lesson. When fear makes you tremble, have faith in God. Lift up hands that hang down. Strengthen feeble knees. Take courage. If God is for you, nothing can be against you—not even the Goliath of death. That enemy was defeated the second the heart began to beat in Jesus's lifeless body as it lay in that cold tomb.

Our battle is not against flesh and blood. Satan is the god of this world—the one who came to kill, steal, and destroy. And just as David rejected the armor of Saul, so we say that "the weapons of our warfare are not carnal but mighty in God for pulling down strongholds" (2 Cor. 10:4). One of these weapons is the shield of trust in God.

When you go to share your faith and the Goliath of fear taunts you, use your faith. Trust in the Lord with all your heart. Say with the psalmist, "The LORD is my helper; I will not fear" (Heb. 13:6). That's the first principle of the Christian walk.

The second lesson issues from the first. This lesson gives us the impetus to use faith effectively. A retired police officer once told me that when he and his fellow officers were approaching an armed criminal, they would each want to go in first. He said they had no fear. But this same manly looking, tough ex-cop told me he wanted to open-air preach but was terrified. He asked what he should do, so I shared the following analogy.

You are at a friend's house, sitting by his swimming pool on a hot day. You have been hesitant to dive in because it's not a heated pool. You know that when you hit the water, your flesh is going to feel it. You find yourself standing on the pool's edge looking at the cold water. Your friends call out that the water is fine and encourage you to dive in. The longer you stand there, the harder it becomes.

Now consider a second scenario of the same scene. You are seated by the pool and you see your toddler run to the water's edge, fall into the swimming pool, and sink to the bottom. Do you think about the cold water? Not for a second. Do you need the coaxing of your friends? Of course not. You immediately dive in and grab that precious child!

How did you overcome fear? The answer is simple: love. Your love for your child immediately dealt with your frivolous concern about the cold water.

The key to reaching those who are perishing in their sins is love. It casts out all fear. If you are afraid to share your faith, don't pray for less fear. Pray for more love. That is what is missing. And that thought calls out modern Christendom. They see the child drowning and deliberately busy themselves folding towels and preparing drinks.

The Bible uses an even more fearful picture when it paints the fate of the lost. It doesn't use water; it uses fire: "And on some have compassion, making a distinction; but others save with fear, pulling them out of the fire, hating even the garment defiled by the flesh" (Jude 22–23). Notice the presence of love in this verse: "And on some have compassion." Love cannot sit in passivity. It must take action.

The Motivation

We find the motivation to reach the lost in our God-given conscience. The human conscience is like a compass needle that points toward the north. When it does its duty, the conscience stubbornly points toward righteousness, and righteousness points to life.

I couldn't live with myself if I allowed a child to drown in a swimming pool or if I allowed someone to burn to death without trying to help them.

The world often treats the conscience as the enemy of pleasure or, at the least, as an annoying party pooper. As Christians, we should look on our conscience as the battery in a smoke detector. It should send out a loud alarm if we are doing something that is morally wrong. It's morally wrong to busy ourselves with other things while anyone goes to hell.

If I walk past any human being without concern for their salvation, an alarm bell goes off. A loud one. I immediately hear God whispering, "There used to be a time when I could trust you." That thought unnerves me. It's a slap in my unloving face. It wakes me up. I'm letting the child drown. Never once have I regretted going back and sharing the gospel.

STUDY QUESTIONS

1. Why do you think so few Christians have a deep concern for the lost?
2. Explain why addressing the many worthy social issues is not the goal of the church.
3. What word did Spurgeon use to describe the task of evangelism? Why is it such an annoying task?
4. What are your greatest fears when it comes to sharing the gospel?
5. What was David's motivation in his fight with Goliath?
6. Do you ever have trouble trusting God?
7. Would it insult you if someone said they had trouble trusting you? Why?

More Important Than Apologetics

Someone can have their questions answered about suffering, the existence of God, and all the other big issues and still end up in hell. God forbid we should ever facilitate that. Our aim should be to present the gospel in an understandable way so that sinners will be saved from God's wrath. It would be a vain and tragic exercise indeed to answer a man's every question about a parachute and then watch him jump without it.

When David went into battle with Goliath, he took five smooth stones and his trusty sling. The stones would have been useless without that sling. The sling gave thrust and direction to his stones. Are you walking into battle with a sling?

The Sling

The Los Angeles airport is never fun. There are just too many people.

A friend and I were waiting for a flight when a man in his early thirties sat down next to me. We didn't acknowledge each other's existence. He, no doubt, didn't enjoy sitting in the cattle car, and he, no doubt, didn't want to talk to some stranger. The more I thought about talking to him about his salvation, the more fearful I felt. Goliath was taunting me.

He was clutching his phone, so I ignored my negative thoughts and said, "How did we live without phones?" He looked at me and nodded in agreement. I then asked what he did for a living. He was a lawyer. "You don't look like one," I commented.

He looked down at his loose T-shirt. As he smiled, I asked where he was headed. "New York," he replied.

His wife, sitting on the other side of him, then said, "He's going to run in the New York marathon."

I was genuinely impressed. We introduced ourselves, and I asked a stack of questions. I had found his sweet spot, and he seemed to enjoy answering every question.

After chatting for about five minutes, I took courage and said, "Nate, I've got a question for you. Do you think there's an afterlife?" This was my door-open-door-close moment.

He said, "I don't know. I do hope so."

His answer welcomed me in.

"If Heaven exists, are you going there? Are you a good person?"

He answered that he thought he was, and that's when I said, "You're a lawyer. I'm going to be your prosecutor. You defend yourself, and let's see if you're good enough." He smiled.

"How many lies have you told in your life?"

"Many."

"Have you ever stolen anything, even something small?"

"X$@!, yes."

"Have you ever used God's name in vain?"

"Yes." He had just used it seconds earlier.

"Jesus said whoever looks at a woman with lust has committed adultery already with her in his heart. Have you looked at a woman this way?"

"Yes, at my wife."

"Anyone else?"

He hesitated. "Yes."

"Nate, I'm not judging you, but you've just admitted to me that you are a lying, thieving, blasphemous adulterer at heart. On judgment day, will God find you to be innocent or guilty?"

"Guilty."

"Heaven or hell?"

Nate admitted that he was heading for hell and that the fact did concern him. I took the time to share the glorious gospel with him—that we broke God's law, the Ten Commandments, and Jesus paid our fine on the cross. Nate listened intently and even took literature from me that he said he would read.

Can you see the sling that gave the gospel its thrust? It was the moral law. The Ten Commandments gave Nate the knowledge that he had sinned against God and that he was in big trouble. The law made the gospel make sense. Charles Spurgeon said, "The Law is for the self-righteous, to humble their pride: the gospel is for the lost, to remove their despair."[1]

But something else took place in the airport. It is another vital key, and it's one that has opened thousands of doors for me over the years. It has calmed my fears and given me courage. I rarely begin a witnessing conversation without it.

I hope I've teased you enough to make sure that you listen to what this is, because I don't want you to miss it.

I said to Nate, "Do you think there's an afterlife?"

That question was not only the key to inoffensively opening a conversation about the things of God but also the key to dealing with my fears. I was able to initiate talk about God without mentioning sin, judgment day, Heaven, hell, or repentance. All I did was ask his opinion about the afterlife. That's the favorite subject of most people—our opinion. When someone asks for it, we feel a sense of importance.

That one question is precious to me. For years I struggled with how to open a spiritual conversation with a stranger. The mole hill of starting a conversation would become a mountain as I sat next to a stranger on a plane. "Do you think there's an afterlife?" was an instant mountain mover.

Twelve-Year Collection

The Evidence Bible is filled with my favorite apologetical arguments. For twelve years I collected every thought, argument, quote, and anecdote in the front of my Bible until it was pregnant with truth. I'm a big believer in apologetics.

One of my favorite Bible teachers speaks about how to defend the faith. He is so eloquent and has such a brilliant mind that it makes me never want to open my mouth again. I'm not intellectually worthy to wash his socks. Plus, he is incredibly gracious and humble. I say this because I want you to know that what I'm going to say next is not a criticism. It simply illustrates a very important point when it comes to sharing our faith.

In brief, he speaks about the importance of truth when reasoning with the unsaved. When testing truth, there are two theories—the correspondence theory and the coherence theory. Also, consistency, empirical adequacy, and existential relevance must be considered. Questions regarding our origin, meaning, morality, and destiny must be dealt with, and to do so we must pull together five disciplines—theology, epistemology, metaphysics, ethics, and anthropology.

Got it? Are you now ready to take up the task of apologetics? If you did get it, you're smarter than me, because what he said went way over my head. Or you may be like me and have trouble understanding all those concepts. I know my intellectual limitations, so when sharing the gospel, I simply do what Jesus did: use the Ten Commandments to stir the conscience and show sinners they need the Savior.

If you watch our witnessing videos, you'll notice that I rarely get into arguments about the infallibility of Scripture, the deity of Christ, evolution, why there is suffering, and other difficult subjects.[2] When I do occasionally enter that territory, I am always aware that there is an easy way out, and I take that exit because of expediency. I'm heading for the cross. I don't want mountains or valleys to slow me down or send me in another direction. I can exit the highway of apologetics at any time, because I have learned the importance of having control of the direction I take.

Suppose we study apologetics because we want to be able to debate with those who are contentious when it comes to the inspiration of Scripture. Let's, therefore, surmise that you believe that our faith rests on the credibility of Holy Scripture, and you desire to arm yourself with evidence that will convince the skeptic that its stories are credible. Take, for example, the often-mocked story of Noah's ark. The world doesn't believe it was built nor that animals boarded it two by two. So you have readied yourself with apologetics to defend the Bible. You convince the skeptic that it is possible to fit all the animals into a ship—if it's large enough and the animals aren't fully grown, that the rain could have flooded the entire earth and covered all the mountains, and that there is existing and adequate archaeological evidence to back up a worldwide flood.

You did it! He nods in affirmation that what didn't make any sense to him before now seems credible. The once skeptical sinner now believes that Noah did build an ark. But he's not yet come to Christ, so you have more work to do. Your next job is to convince him that a big fish swallowed a man, that he stayed alive for three days (or perhaps he died and was resurrected after three days), and that he was spat out on the shore. Then you must convince him that Lot's wife literally turned into a pillar of salt and that Samson's strength was in his hair and he killed one thousand men with the jawbone of a donkey. After that you will need to persuade him that a snake (a serpent) spoke to Eve. Then you will present your case for the stopping of the sun, walls falling down with a shout, water turning to blood, the sea opening up, a donkey speaking with a man's voice, water turning to wine, and a thousand and one other stories that make Rapunzel and her hair, Cinderella and her pumpkin, and Pinocchio and his big nose almost seem credible.

While we are called to "defend" the faith, it is a good strategy to also try to "advance" it. It is unwise to joust with a sword and never use it to win the fight. To "win" the fight is to convince sinners they are in mortal and eternal danger and desperately need the Savior. Our ultimate goal is not to convince anyone that the Bible is credible. Even the devil knows that. Our churches are full of people who believe that the Bible is the Word of God, but they've never obeyed its command to repent and trust alone in the Savior. They haven't seen their terrible danger, more than likely because they were never "instructed out of the law" (Rom. 2:18).

Jesus didn't say to go into all the world and try to convince them that the strange stories in the Bible are true. He said to "go into all the world and preach the gospel to every creature" (Mark 16:15). The gospel is the power of God to salvation (see Rom. 1:16). The gospel takes the sword to the heart. If we believe that our agenda is to convince the world in their intellect, we are putting the cart before the horse.

We will get nowhere.

I want to leave you with two illustrations and one incredible story that show how effective the moral law is in our task of sharing the gospel and defending our faith.

Back to the Sword Fight

In one of the most famous fight scenes in the Indiana Jones movies, the hero is being attacked by a fearsome man with a lethal-looking sword. I haven't seen the whole movie, but I certainly remember seeing this part. The attacker is amazingly adept with the razor-sharp weapon, moving it through the air with lightning speed like some sort of sideshow juggler. The hero is feet in front of him, and it looks like all is over for him—he's armed with only a leather whip. When it looks like certain curtains for Mr. Jones, he casually pulls out a gun from his jacket pocket and shoots the swordsman through the heart. It was all over with one shot. It made the enemy look ridiculous, because despite all the hoopla, he was simply out-weaponed. A sword is useless in the face of a speeding bullet.

The Ten Commandments outgun the enemy. He has a sharp sword, but we have ten great cannons. Those cannons are mighty through God for the immediate shooting down of strongholds.

Fishers of Men

If I wanted to teach you how to fish, I could take you to a nice little pond and let you catch a nice little fish. But I'd rather take you deep-sea fishing and let you experience some real action.

When a deep-sea fisherman gets a marlin on his line, he will let it run. He does this because he knows that at any time he chooses, he can jerk back the rod and get the hook deeper into the jaw.

The hook that Jesus used was the moral law, and the jaw is the sinner's conscience. Because I know this, I can let the person to whom I'm speaking run off in any direction they want. Any time I choose, I can take complete control. I simply ask the question "Do you think you're a good person?" and bring out the big-gun commandments as Jesus did in Mark 10:17–19:

> Now as He was going out on the road, one came running, knelt before Him, and asked Him, "Good Teacher, what shall I do that I may inherit eternal life?"

So Jesus said to him, "Why do you call Me good? No one is good but One, that is, God. You know the commandments: 'Do not commit adultery,' 'Do not murder,' 'Do not steal,' 'Do not bear false witness,' 'Do not defraud,' 'Honor your father and your mother.'"

Using the moral law like Jesus did gives me a level playing field, because I'm not talking to the sinner's contentious intellect. I have moved to his conscience. This puts even Einstein at a disadvantage. If I'm speaking to someone's intellect, they respond with the intellect. They are in control. But if I'm speaking to their conscience, it does the talking: "Who show the work of the law written in their hearts, their conscience also bearing witness, and between themselves their thoughts accusing or else excusing them" (Rom. 2:15).

When You See Sea Fog

I'm not a fan of sea fog. One moment you're having a nice day at the beach, and the next moment fog comes from nowhere and steals the warmth and light of the sun. Instead of blue sky, there is nothing but gloom, dampness, and cold air. When I go to Huntington Beach each Saturday to preach the gospel, I keep a jacket in reserve so that I'm never caught off guard by the fog.

If you're a Christian with a desire to reach the lost, you should know that the enemy will often send the sea fog of discouragement your way. Of course, we know that the fog doesn't remove the warmth and light of the sun; it just hides it. And we know that discouragement doesn't remove the warmth and light of the love of God; it too just hides it. We need to keep the jacket of faith handy for when the fog comes.

Ray Comfort

That "jacket" is the knowledge that our labor is never in vain. We are, therefore, never discouraged by a lack of visual results. Always keep in mind that when we share the gospel, we are scattering precious seed. Only God knows the soil on which it lands.

I received a phone call in late 2017 from a trucker named Steve. He told me that back in 2009, he had found a teaching CD of mine called "Hell's Best Kept Secret" and listened to it in his truck. The CD expounds the biblical principle we've been looking into—the necessity of preceding the message of the gospel with the law of God. Again, we do this because it's what Jesus and the apostles did. We should follow their example and open up the Ten Commandments to give the sinner the knowledge of sin before we speak of God's love expressed in the cross. This was the principle used by the great preachers of the past such as Charles Spurgeon, John Wesley, and George Whitefield.

When Hosea 4:6 is read in context, it shows that the law is the knowledge of sin, without which people perish:

> My people are destroyed for lack of knowledge [of My law, where I reveal My will]. Because you [the priestly nation] have rejected knowledge, I will also reject you from being My priest. Since you have forgotten the law of your God, I will also forget your children. (AMP)

If we reject the moral law, we are left without the knowledge of sin—and why should anyone repent and trust in Christ if they have no knowledge of sin? The gospel's call to repent and trust the Savior is meaningless and foolish without the light of God's law to show the need for grace.

In Luke 11:52, Jesus rebuked the lawyers. They were not criminal lawyers but professed to be experts in God's law. Yet they failed to use the His law to show sin to be "exceedingly sinful" (Rom. 7:13). He called it the "key of knowledge," because its function is to bring the knowledge of sin: "Woe to you lawyers! *For you have taken away the key of knowledge.* You did not enter in yourselves, and those who were entering in you hindered" (Luke 11:52, emphasis added). They twisted the key out of shape with their vain traditions, so that it wouldn't do what it was intended to do—to act as a schoolmaster to bring sinners to Christ (see Gal. 3:24).

Steve the trucker was impressed with what he heard on the CD, so when he dropped into a truck repair shop in Cincinnati, he shared the gospel (using the law) with a mechanic who was working on a truck. However, the man was unresponsive. It seemed that the principle didn't work.

A short time later, another mechanic approached Steve and said that while he was talking to the first mechanic, he had been under the truck repairing it. He said that he hung on to every word that Steve said and was so overcome with conviction he stopped working, went outside, and yielded his life to Christ.

Never let the fog of discouragement settle on you. Your labor is never in vain.

STUDY QUESTIONS

1. What is the biblical agenda of the church?
2. Explain the relationship of the sling to a stone and how that pertains to the moral law and the gospel.

Ray Comfort

3. Name three very strange Bible stories.

4. What did we learn from the Indiana Jones analogy?

5. What was the hook (and what was the jaw) in the fishing analogy?

6. Where in Scripture did Jesus use the law to bring the knowledge of sin?

7. Name three great preachers who advocated this biblical principle.

1. "If God is supposed to be in control of the world, why does it seem so out of control?"

The world doesn't just seem out of control. It is out of control. It's a mess in every area. Nations are rising against nations. There are wars and rumors of wars. There is violence in homes and in the workplace. Human beings murder human beings every day. Women are raped, people are kidnapped, sex slaves are taken, children are molested, kids are bullied, and banks are robbed. There is corruption in politics, in law enforcement, in the pulpit, and in every area of society. There are devastating hurricanes, droughts, famines, floods, mudslides, tsunamis, tornadoes, and earthquakes. We have epidemics of alcoholism, school shootings, drug addiction, and suicide. Marriages are shattered, children are scarred, people are lonely, and multitudes are plagued by all kinds of fears. There are unending cancerous diseases plaguing humanity. It has become normal and expected to have killer flu "seasons" each year. The *New York Times* reports:

> Even in a mild year, flu kills about 12,000 Americans, the C.D.C. estimates. In a bad year, it kills up to 56,000. . . .

And, every season, flu and its complications, including pneumonia, meningitis and sepsis, kill some apparently healthy people.[1]

On top of all this, millions suffer from arthritis, back pain, joint pain, blindness, deafness, and of course, chronic depression—which is understandable, because all these terrible things are happening every day somewhere in this sad, old world. And we've looked at only the tiny tip of the massive and cold iceberg of the human tragedy. These things must show us that either God isn't in control, or He doesn't have His hands firmly on the steering wheel.

Those who ask the question we're currently considering are often the ones who are known as *unbelievers*. Unbelievers are called unbelievers because they don't believe the biblical explanation of why these things are so, or maybe they have never heard it. They are looking for an explanation for the chaos they see in the world.

Two Important Points

Whatever the case, there are two important points to make when answering this question. The first point is that the Bible tells us "in the beginning," when God created all things, He looked at everything He had made and it was all very good. There were none of these terrible happenings then. It was Utopia—heaven on earth. There was no disease, pain, suffering, or death. Nor was there any evil on earth. But Adam sinned against God, and with sin came the "fall," which ushered in evil and its bedbugs of disease, suffering, and death.

To those who believe the Bible, every human suffering is recognized as the result of living in the fallen creation detailed in Genesis. There is no mystery about this, because we have the perfect explanation from God Himself.

For those who don't believe the biblical explanation, suffering, disease, pain, and death are dark mysteries. And so they are plagued with the question why, couched in the accusation that God is incompetent.

Still others don't ask this question. They live day in and day out in this fallen world, see all the horrors, and conclude that this was the way God planned it. They are destined to be deeply disillusioned with both their image of God and life itself.

This brings us to the second point to be made when answering the current question. The Bible tells us that although God is the Creator of all things and is sovereign over everything, Satan is the god of this world:

> Therefore, since we have this ministry, as we have received mercy, we do not lose heart. But we have renounced the hidden things of shame, not walking in craftiness nor handling the word of God deceitfully, but by manifestation of the truth commending ourselves to every[one's] conscience in the sight of God. But even if our gospel is veiled, it is veiled to those who are perishing, whose minds the god of this age has blinded, who do not believe, lest the light of the gospel of the glory of Christ, who is the image of God, should shine on them. (2 Cor. 4:1–4)

Notice that the god of this world blinds the minds of those "who do not believe." If they simply believed the gospel, they would be compelled to repent and trust the Savior.

They would no longer be in darkness. They would know the truth, and the truth would set them free.

When it comes to salvation, belief is pivotal: "For since, in the wisdom of God, the world through wisdom did not know God, it pleased God through the foolishness of the message preached to save *those who believe*" (1 Cor. 1:21, emphasis added).

The Hope of the Gospel

God in His sovereignty (and through His permissive will) allows all the miseries that come to humanity. But these things are not His perfect will. His perfect will is coming in the form of the literal kingdom of God. Jesus told us, in what is commonly called "The Lord's Prayer," to pray for that coming kingdom: "Thy Kingdom come, Thy will be done in earth, as it is in heaven" (Matt. 6:10 KJV). Every believer has this glorious hope of the coming new world.

There will be a new Heaven and a new earth, where there will be no evil and where God's perfect will will be done. There will be no disease, pain, suffering, or death. Animals will not devour each other. The wolf will lie down with the lamb, and nations will dwell in peace and safety, because they have submitted to the lordship of the God who gave them life.

There will be no more war, no fear of the future, no sorrow, and best of all, there will be no more death. Scripture tells us that God Himself will wipe away all tears from the eyes of humanity, and we will have "pleasure forevermore" (Ps. 16:11). What a wonderful and glorious hope believers have, all because of God's amazing kindness. But the unbeliever doesn't have this hope, because he refuses to simply believe. He stands on his own oxygen hose. The world is chaotic and out of control, because people refuse to trust God.

In a world that is out of control, our message to unbelievers is that they should give God control of their lives. Give God life's steering wheel. Trust Him, and then take a back seat and relax. The first step is simply to believe the warnings of Scripture, repent, and then "put on the Lord Jesus Christ" (Rom. 13:14). It all starts with a mustard seed of belief: "Whoever believes in the Son has eternal life, but whoever rejects the Son will not see life, for God's wrath remains on them" (John 3:36 NIV).

STUDY QUESTIONS

1. Name ten disastrous things that show us that this is a fallen world.
2. How would you describe an unbeliever?
3. How would you describe life before the fall?
4. Who is "the god of this world," and what does he do to unbelievers?
5. What is promised in the coming kingdom of God?
6. What is it that will lie down with the lamb?
7. Why is belief so important?

2. "What sort of God would threaten to torture people in hell forever just because they don't believe in Him?" (Part One)

This is a legitimate question. How can hell be reconciled with a God who is love and who is good as the Bible says? To answer this, we will back up and look at some old news. In 1990, the *New York Times* published an article that headlined, "Prison for 3 Northwest Pilots Who Flew Jet While Drunk."

> MINNEAPOLIS, Oct. 26—Three former Northwest Airlines pilots who flew a passenger jet while intoxicated were sentenced to prison today, two for a year and the other for 16 months. The sentences were within Federal guidelines, which recommended 12 to 18 months; the maximum would have been 15 years. The three were convicted of being intoxicated while flying a Boeing 727 with 91 passengers from Fargo, N.D., to Minneapolis the morning of March 8. As he announced his decision, Judge Rosenbaum said he was particularly disturbed that all three pilots had been under the influence. "Who can comprehend an entire crew

alcohol-impaired?" The judge said their actions amounted to a breach of faith with the traveling public. "It is a crime against our sense of security," he said. "In that sense, all of us are a victim of this crime."[1]

The airlines and the public trusted these pilots, but they didn't take that trust seriously. God Himself has entrusted us with the gospel, so this is a task we must soberly approach with the utmost fear and trembling. The people who ask our current question are actually asking who our God is—they don't understand His character. And God has entrusted us with the task of telling these questioners who He is.

The Glory of God

I'm forever fascinated by the universal way we express joy. Place a cute kitten in front of a baby and watch his hands. He can hardly sit up by himself, yet he claps his hands in glee as he looks on what delights his little heart. Then watch eighty thousand adults clap with a similar glee because they see something that delights them on a sporting field. There is something magical about the applause and roar of a massive crowd.

When my eldest son was four years old, I thought of a way to make the crucifixion real to him. I called the manager of a local movie theater and asked if I could bring my son into the theater for the last thirty minutes of the movie *Ben Hur*, which was screening at the time. The manager was very congenial, and so my son and I sat down in the theater to watch the crucifixion. Keep in mind that this was in 1976, and the only screen my boy had seen was a fourteen-inch black-and-white television set. And we were in a movie theater called "Cinerama." This entailed three huge screens and the new phenomenon of "surround sound."

As we watched the crucifixion, I whispered to him that there was going to be thunder and lightning any moment. Suddenly, there was a massive boom and a flash of lightning, and he screamed, "Let's get out of here!" I immediately picked him up in my arms, and we ran out of the theater.

Realistic though surround sound may be, we cannot duplicate the atmosphere of a roaring crowd. If you have ever felt it, you know why so many pay so much to sit like frozen sardines in a cold stadium. They could see the same game at home on a big-screen TV with a modern sound system while sitting in their favorite armchair. But they pack into that stadium because it's amazing to feel the atmosphere of a crowd as it gives glory, honor, and praise to another human being. It's glorious in the truest sense of the word.

The first time I felt that atmosphere, I couldn't help but think of the redeemed giving glory, honor, and praise to God around His throne. We see through a glass darkly when we have such thoughts, although Scripture does give us some light:

> The four living creatures, each having six wings, were full of eyes around and within. And they do not rest day or night, saying:
>
>> "Holy, holy, holy,
>> Lord God Almighty,
>> Who was and is and is to come!"
>
> Whenever the living creatures give glory and honor and thanks to Him who sits on the throne, who lives forever and

ever, the twenty-four elders fall down before Him who sits on the throne and worship Him who lives forever and ever, and cast their crowns before the throne, saying:

> "You are worthy, O Lord,
> To receive glory and honor and power;
> For You created all things,
> And by Your will they exist and were created."
> (Rev. 4:8–11)

We can only imagine the unspeakably glorious atmosphere of God's immediate presence. But as we do so, we should follow the example of the four living creatures who cried, "Holy, holy, holy," and never separate the spectacle of His glory from His holiness. To try to separate the glory of God from the holiness of God is like trying to separate the sun from its heat. A glorious sunrise is a thing of serene beauty. But glorious though it may be, if we fell onto the face of the sun, we would be instantly consumed by its terrifying heat.

Moses once asked to see the brightness of God's glory. He wanted to have a close look at the sunrise. But God told him that he couldn't see it and live. Moses would be instantly consumed by His holiness. The Bible warns, "Our God is a *consuming fire*" (Heb. 12:29, emphasis added).

Think of a good judge. Before him stands a guilty and unrepentant criminal. He smiles wickedly as the judge informs him that he has been found guilty of raping and then cutting the throats of three innocent teenage girls. To bring a measure of empathy into this scenario, think of one of those girls as your sister or perhaps a daughter. That's what a good judge would do. He would enter into the pain of the families who have suffered such a terrible loss.

As the judge speaks, his hands shake with anger at the embodiment of evil before him. He can't wait to bring his gavel down in wrath—and it's his goodness that motivates his wrath. His anger is in direct proportion to his goodness. If he wasn't angry, he wouldn't be good. He would be a cold-hearted human being who shouldn't be sitting as a judge.

Look at what God said would pass in front of Moses after he asked to see His glory:

> Then [God] said, "I will make all *My goodness* pass before you, and I will proclaim the name of the LORD before you. I will be gracious to whom I will be gracious, and I will have compassion on whom I will have compassion." But He said, "You cannot see My face; for no [one] shall see Me, and live." And the LORD said, "Here is a place by Me, and you shall stand on the rock. So it shall be, while My glory passes by, that I will put you in the cleft of the rock, and will cover you with My hand while I pass by. Then I will take away My hand, and you shall see My back; but My face shall not be seen." (Exod. 33:19–23, emphasis added)

At first this seems a little strange. Moses asked to see God's glory, and God responds by saying that He would pass His goodness before him. This is because His glory and His goodness cannot be separated. If Moses had stood directly before God's goodness rather than in the cleft of the rock, the wrath of God would have consumed him in an instant because of his sin. Like that judge before the evil criminal, God's hand longs to bring down the gavel on all evil. The only way sinners could ever stand in His presence and see His glory without being consumed would be if we were pure of heart. Jesus said, "Blessed are the pure in heart, for they shall see God"

Ray Comfort

(Matt. 5:8), and it's Jesus who has made us pure by His blood. We have been hidden in Christ. He is our rock, our shelter:

> Rock of Ages, cleft for me,
> Let me hide myself in Thee;
> Let the water and the blood,
> From Thy wounded side which flowed,
> Be of sin the double cure,
> Save from wrath and make me pure.[2]

As we stand before the throne of almighty God, we are going to see the One who formed our eyes and ears and the blood that flows through our myriad of veins. We are going to see the maker of every bird and animal, every living tree and its fruits, of thunder and lightning, the sun, moon and stars, and night and day.

We are going to see Him who created the tiny body of a baby and then inhabited that body to suffer for our sins. God was in Christ reconciling the world to Himself. At the same time, He was demonstrating His love for us, in that, while we were still sinners Christ died for us as the sacrificial Lamb. It is before His throne that we will cry in a loud voice, "Worthy is the Lamb who was slain to receive power and riches and wisdom, and strength and honor and glory and blessing" (Rev. 5:12).

How could evil exist in the presence of such holiness? The answer is that it can't.

Blinding Glory

The only reason we can look at a sunrise is because we look at it through the earth's atmosphere. If we stared at it, even for a moment, at high noon, its glory would blind us. But because it sinks low on the earth, we can admire its amazing beauty.

Almighty God came low through the incarnation so that we could see His glory. Second Corinthians 4:6 says that Jesus came to give us "the light of the knowledge of the glory of God in the face of Jesus Christ." Hebrews 1:3 tells us that Jesus was "the brightness of [God's] glory, and the express image of His person." And John 1:14, also speaking of Jesus, says, "And the Word became flesh and dwelt among us, and we beheld His glory, the glory as of the only begotten of the Father, full of grace and truth."

But as we look at Jesus and admire the glorious attributes of His amazing love, meekness, humility, gentleness, and kindness, we must never forget the attributes of His holiness and fearful wrath. The harmless Lamb is coming back as a roaring lion "when the Lord Jesus is revealed from heaven with His mighty angels, in flaming fire taking vengeance on those who do not know God, and on those who do not obey the gospel of our Lord Jesus Christ" (2 Thess. 1:7–9).

Once we catch a glimpse of the holiness of God, the existence of hell becomes a most necessary conclusion. If God is good, He must be angry at evil and He must have a place of punishment for those who do evil. Ask any person with a semblance of right and wrong what Hitler's eternal fate should be. Should he go to Heaven or hell? The thought that there might be no judgment for his heinous crimes is disgusting. If his punishment was merely a self-inflicted shot to the head, then he suffered no more than the average person who dies. But those who know what he did to the Jews and other tragic victims of the Holocaust will almost always concede that he should go to hell.

The question "What sort of God would threaten to torture people in hell forever just because they don't believe in Him?" can be summarized to "How could a God who is good create hell?" But when we consider God's goodness and His glory, the question should be further changed to "How could a God who is good *not* create hell?" A. W. Tozer said, "The vague and tenuous hope that God is too kind to punish the ungodly has become a deadly opiate for the consciences of millions."[3]

When it comes to admitting sin, I have discovered that people are reluctant and predictable. They will say God is not that good, and sin isn't that bad. The common answer to "How many lies have you told in your life?" is that yes, they have lied, but they were just small lies when they were children. They have also stolen but only as a child, and they were just little things. They claim these are small sins, not big sins; they are trivial misdemeanors that barely deserve a rap on the knuckles. And that would be the case if God was like they imagine Him to be.

But He's nothing like they imagine Him to be—not even slightly.

To be continued.

3. "What sort of God would threaten to torture people in hell forever just because they don't believe in Him?" (Part Two)

The glory of God isn't restricted to His immediate presence; it is manifest in different forms. When Jesus was about to raise Lazarus from the dead, He said that those present were about to see the glory of God: "Jesus said to her, 'Did I not say to you that if you would believe you would see the glory of God?'" (John 11:40). When the shepherds were keeping watch over their flock at night, we are told, "And behold, an angel of the Lord stood before them, and the glory of the Lord shone around them, and they were greatly afraid" (Luke 2:9). Psalm 19:1 says that "the heavens declare the glory of God" in the same way a painting expresses the character and ability of a painter.

However, the ungodly see His works but refuse to give Him any praise or thanksgiving: "Because that, when they knew God, they glorified him not as God, neither were thankful; but became vain in their imaginations, and their foolish heart was darkened" (Rom. 1:21 KJV).

Sinners bring God down and lift man up. They give praise to nature rather than the Creator, and then they imagine that He doesn't think sin is serious. The Scriptures, however, warn that in His holy eyes, lying, stealing, lust, hatred, blasphemy, adultery, fornication, greed, rebellion, and a thousand other sins are extremely serious. Divine justice cries out for retribution, and hell makes perfect sense. It is frighteningly reasonable.

The bottom line is that if God is good, He must see that perfect justice is done. But the Bible also says that God is love. Surely His love would stay His hand when it comes to hell. How could a God who is the very essence and reservoir of love send anyone to hell?

But the fact that He is love is irrelevant when it comes to His justice. A judge may be the most loving of men, but when he is called to administer justice to a vicious murderer, he puts his love aside. His emotions must not influence his judgment. Look at the judicial oath for a US judge:

> "I, ___ ___, do solemnly swear (or affirm) that I will administer justice without respect to persons, and do equal right to the poor and to the rich, and that I will faithfully and impartially discharge and perform all the duties incumbent upon me as ___ under the Constitution and laws of the United States. So help me God."[1]

A judge must be impartial. He must never be swayed by a criminal's fame, political status, personal charisma, or celebrity. If he admires and even loves a famous personality, he must set that aside. A good judge will tell jurors to defer their emotions and look only at the evidence when making a judgment. This is why justice is internationally depicted as a blindfolded woman holding the scales of justice.

In her right hand, Lady Justice is seen to have a sword that faces downwards. This sword represents punishment. This sword is held below the scales to show that evidence and court is always held before punishment. . . .

The blindfold represents objectivity, in that justice is or should be meted out objectively, without any fear or favor, regardless of money, wealth, power, or identity; blind justice and impartiality. . . .

In her left hand, Lady Justice holds balance scales, which represent the weighing of evidence. When taken with the blindfold, the symbolism is that evidence must be weighed on its own merit.[2]

The Bible says, "God shows no partiality" (Acts 10:34). He is not swayed in the slightest by wealth, charisma, power, or celebrity. The day will come when He sets aside His love, rich in mercy though He may be, and puts on the fearful black cap of wrath and passes terrifying judgment on all who have violated His perfect law. Consider Psalm 96:11–13:

> Let the heavens rejoice, and let the earth be glad;
> Let the sea roar, and all its fullness;
> Let the field be joyful, and all that is in it.
> Then all the trees of the woods will rejoice before
>   the LORD.
> For He is coming, for He is coming to judge the
>   earth.
> He shall judge the world with righteousness,
> And the peoples with His truth.

Here, the Bible uses personification to tell us that nature rejoices with great joy at the thought of judgment day.

There was a lawless cowboy town in Texas in the early 1800s where every day women were raped, people were murdered, and banks were robbed because there was no law in the town. The sheriff had been murdered, and no one would take his place.

The good people of the town formed a committee and hired the famous Texas Rangers, who had formed together in 1823 to defend Texas after the Mexican War of Independence. These ten rangers actually existed, and they became the West's most famous lawmen, killing many outlaws, including the notorious bank robber Sam Bass.

The lawless town's judgment day was coming. Who would be fearful of that day? Only the criminals. Who would rejoice? The good people of the town.

And that's why God's judgment day is a fearful thing for humanity. We are sinful by nature, and the knowledge of our guilt produces fear at the very thought of God's judgment. Listen to Psalm 98:7–9:

> Let the sea roar, and all its fullness,
> The world and those who dwell in it;
> Let the rivers clap their hands;
> Let the hills be joyful together before the LORD,
> For He is coming to judge the earth.
> With righteousness He shall judge the world,
> And the peoples with equity.

Oh, the day is coming when Hitler and every wicked Nazi gets justice. What a day of rejoicing that will be. But when we consider the holiness of God, our hearts should tremble for the rest of humanity.

Such a thought should make us further tremble, because we have been entrusted by God Himself with the everlasting gospel.

When I go somewhere to preach to the unsaved, I am going somewhere I don't want to go, to say something I don't want to say, to people who don't want to hear it. But because hell exists, I tremble. I know that, like every other Christian, I must warn the lost of hell's existence. I have a sobering moral obligation. Shame on me if I don't. Woe to me if I won't: "For if I preach the gospel, I have nothing to boast of, for necessity is laid upon me; yes, woe is me if I do not preach the gospel!" (1 Cor. 9:16).

Without the help of God, the task we have of preaching the gospel to a God-hating, sin-loving, idolatrous world would be impossible. But take heart, dear Christian; He hasn't left us without help. We have been given weapons of warfare that are not carnal but mighty through God to the pulling down of strongholds. By His power, we will tell the world of His power.

Two Necessary Elements of Gospel Proclamation

The most eloquent of apologists may be able to convince their hearers that God is real, that the Bible is His Word, and that Jesus is the only Savior, and yet they still remain unsaved. They will stay in their sins until they repent and trust alone in Jesus. Our aim, therefore, as those who preach the everlasting gospel, is not to see people intellectually convinced of the gospel but to see people partake in it.

Statistics tell us that we are not reaching this dying world as we should.[3] We are not reaching the lost because two necessary elements are being left out of modern gospel proclamation. The first omission is a failure to inform the world of the nature of sin.

Some assume that sinners already understand the nature of sin. Scripture disagrees. Romans 3:11 tells us that "there is none who understands" and "none who seeks after God." The two are tied together: none seek after God because none understand.

It's common for preachers to say that there's something in us that yearns for God. The unsaved try to fill the God-shaped gap in their heart with sports, saving money, sex, and other pursuits. The evangelistic mentality maintains that, though the world may not know it, they are really seeking after God. That's like saying that deep within every criminal is a yearning to seek after the police. The Bible doesn't say that mankind is yearning for and seeking after God. It says that there is none who seek after God. None. Sinners love the darkness and hate the light.

> And this is the condemnation, that the light has come into the world, and [people] loved darkness rather than light, because their deeds were evil. For everyone practicing evil hates the light and does not come to the light, lest [their] deeds should be exposed. (John 3:19–20)

True, God has placed eternity in their hearts (see Eccles. 3:11); they intuitively know they are eternal by nature. But they are not seeking for what they hate. They are yearning for the darkness, not the light.

> God looks down from heaven upon the children of
> men,
> To see if there are any who understand, who seek God.

Every one of them has turned aside;
They have together become corrupt;
There is none who does good,
No, not one. (Ps. 53:2–3)

This darkness must be confronted by God's law. In the parable of the sower (see Matt. 13:3–23; Mark 4:3–20; and Luke 8:4–15), the good-soil hearer is one who hears and understands, and the agent that God gave to bring about the necessary understanding is His moral law. Paul said, "I had not known sin, but by the law" (Rom. 7:7 KJV), and "By the law is the knowledge of sin" (Rom. 3:20). The apostle had no understanding of the nature of sin without the law. Galatians 3:24 (KJV) tells us that the law acts as a "schoolmaster" to bring us to Christ. The function of a schoolmaster is to produce understanding. Sin are the crimes we have committed against God's law (see 1 John 3:4).

When someone dies, the preacher often speaks of the fragility of life and how we need to appreciate it and live it to the fullest. But there is a more important lesson for the living when it comes to the dead. Every death of the offspring of Adam is a sober reminder that God was deadly serious about sin when He said, "The soul who sins shall die" (Ezek. 18:20. But that's not all. The cross is a reminder that God was deadly serious about His love for sinners.

Death is an arresting officer. It will seize upon sinners and drag them in chains before the judge of the universe. Judgment day is the day of their trial, and hell is God's prison. It has no parole. Jesus is the Savior, by whom our case can be dismissed and through whom we escape the damnation of hell. But if sin isn't known to sinners, they think they have committed no crimes. To them, death is merely a part of life, hell is unthinkable, Jesus is irrelevant, and the gospel is foolishness.

If we want sinners to see their need of the Savior, we must expound the law as Jesus did in the Sermon on the Mount and elsewhere. We must faithfully show sin to be exceedingly sinful, and we do that by speaking of the spiritual nature of the law—God requires "truth in the innermost being" (Ps. 51:6 AMP) and sees lust as adultery and hatred as murder. We need to hold high the nature of our Creator and warn complacent sinners that "it is a fearful thing to fall into the hands of the Living God" (Heb. 10:31). We must do as Paul did in Romans 2:19–22, when he said:

> You yourself are . . . an instructor of the foolish, a teacher of babes, having the form of knowledge and truth in the law. You, therefore, who teach another, do you not teach yourself? You who preach that [others] should not steal, do you steal? You who say, "Do not commit adultery," do you commit adultery?

As champions of the moral law, we imitate the Savior by magnifying the law and making it honorable. We also stir that dormant ally in the human heart, the conscience. It is the conscience (which means "with knowledge") that bears witness to the commandments (see Rom. 2:15). A failure to present the law has tragically filled the church with false converts (see *God Has a Wonderful Plan for Your Life* for heartbreaking statistics[4]). This has happened despite the stern warning from men such as Spurgeon, Wesley, Whitefield, and others. They implored the church to use the law to bring the knowledge of sin and said that failure to do so would fill the church with false converts. How can sinners repent if they have no knowledge of sin? Remember, Paul said, "I had not known sin, but by the law." If they don't repent, they will perish, no matter how comfortable they are sitting in the pew.

A friend recently attended a funeral at which the words to "Amazing Grace" were changed slightly to "Amazing grace, how sweet the sound that saved a *person* like me." Those who think they are morally good would find the word *wretch* too strong. But once we understand the absolute holiness of God and that we are children of wrath—drinking wickedness like water, loving the darkness, hating the light, and unthankful and unholy—we know the word *wretch* may not be strong enough.

We may tell the lost that God is holy, but this will mean as much as the word *hot* means to children whom you tell that the sun is hot. They have no way of understanding the heat of twenty-seven million degrees Fahrenheit. But if they stood in front of a large bonfire where they were able to feel the heat from the flames, they would have a tiny measure of understanding of the heat of the sun, because they would now have a way to gauge it.

The way to make *holy* make sense to the lost is to address their conscience rather than their intellect. Through the conscience, they can feel the heat because they have a gauge by which to measure morality. When we expand the spirituality of the law, it shows sinners the nature of their Creator because the law is holy (see Rom. 7:12). May we be reminded of God's holiness every time we glance at the sun.

The gospel makes sense only in light of God's law. Jesus said to go into all the world and preach the gospel to every creature (see Mark 16:15). *Gospel* simply means "good news," and the good news is that Christ died for our sins and rose again on the third day. We broke God's law, and Jesus paid the fine. However, the good news of somebody paying a fine on my behalf will make no sense to me if I don't understand that I have violated the law. If we want the gospel to make sense, we must use the law to bring the knowledge of sin so that the sinner can understand why Christ died. Remember, the true convert "hears the word and understands it" (Matt. 13:23).

Perhaps you've had the experience of driving through your neighborhood and suspecting that a tree or something has been removed because the area looks somehow different. That's what it's like listening to a modern gospel presentation. It takes a sound understanding of the biblical presentation to know what's missing. The next time you hear the gospel preached, listen for the law to bring the knowledge of sin. Listen for the preaching of Christ crucified and the resurrection. Is there a warning of judgment day, the terrible truth of hell, and the necessity of repentance and faith? It's not easy to notice what's not there, but it will help you to make sure that you remember to say what they leave out.

The second omission in modern preaching is connected to the first. It is a failure to preach future punishment by the law. God "commands all people everywhere to repent. For . . . he will judge the world with justice" (Acts 17:30–31 NIV). The righteous standard by which God will judge the world is the moral law (see Rom. 2:12; James 2:12).

The moral law and future punishment are joined at the hip. If we don't use the law to convince sinners that they are law breakers, they will have no fear of being punished. They won't see their need to cleanse their hands or purify their hearts, and their mourning will never be turned to laughter nor their heaviness to joy.

The subject of hell is rarely mentioned from modern pulpits because the message doesn't require it. Jesus is preached, but not as one "who delivers us from the wrath to come" (1 Thess. 1:10). On the other hand, the apostle Paul's motivation for warning the unsaved was the coming wrath. He said, "Knowing, therefore, the terror of the Lord, we persuade" others (2 Cor. 5:11). And the way to persuade others is to tell them that they will be judged by a perfect law. Until they are effectively persuaded, they will stay in their sins within and without Christendom. Workers of iniquity—of lawlessness—sit in the church as weeds among the wheat, foolish virgins among the wise, bad fish among the good, and goats among the sheep, and they will stay there as long as we preach a law-less gospel. They will stay unawakened as long as we talk about the cure but fail to mention the disease. The stone has no power without the sling.

There is an easy fix. Pick up the sling and do what Jesus did. Open up the law regularly, preach future punishment, and mention the existence of hell as Jesus so often did.

We must preface the existence of hell with the evil of sin, or conversations with the lost will not make sense.

Persuading Nico

I was editing a short film called *God-Glorifying Science* when our doorbell rang. I thought the noise was part of the music

I was using in editing, but when I saw my dog lift an ear, I decided to investigate. I peered through the glass window in the wooden front door, and I saw a gentleman looking at something in his hand.

I opened the door, and he introduced himself as Nico and asked if we were customers of a particular company. When I said we weren't, he looked at his chart and read an address. I told him that he had the wrong address. He was embarrassed and said, "I've made a mistake."

I replied that it was no mistake and asked, "Nico, do you think there's an afterlife?"

He did.

"Are you going to make it to Heaven? Are you a good person?"

He said that he thought he was, so I took him through the Ten Commandments. He had broken the seventh, eighth, and ninth, but he said he had never used God's name in vain.

When I asked him if he would be found guilty on judgment day, he said that he didn't believe God was a God of judgment. To him, the very existence of hell was out of the question.

That's when I told him that he had just broken the first and the second of the Ten Commandments. I explained that when we create a god in our own image, we are guilty of idolatry. Then I poured my heart out, telling him of the cross and of my concern for him, and I asked him to judge my motives. I didn't want his money. All I wanted was for him to place his trust in Jesus and find everlasting life. My motivation was his salvation. He was a sinner and heading for hell. It was "knowing the terror of the Lord" that made me earnest in trying to persuade Nico.

He responded, "I still think God doesn't judge people. My god is a god of love."

I said, "Nico, I am so disappointed. You're still holding on to your idol, and it's going to be like a parachute filled with holes. God is nothing like what we imagine Him to be. He is a God of justice, righteousness, holiness, and truth. He has seen your thought life—all those sexual fantasies. Nothing is hidden from His eyes, and every time you sin, you store up His wrath." I thanked him for listening to me and asked him if I could give him a gift. Then I gave him a DVD, a signed book, a movie gift card for our films, and a $5 Subway gift card.

He was very taken aback and said, "I didn't expect to get gifts when I was knocking on doors."

I smiled, shook his hand, and reminded him that he didn't come to our house by mistake.

As Nico walked away, I could see that he was looking at the gifts in his hands. Those small items probably spoke as loud as any sermon. They were tokens of my genuine love and deadly seriousness about where he would spend eternity.

Always keep the axe ready to cut into the stubborn roots of idolatry. Hell is extremely offensive, and creating a false god that has no goodness accommodates the offended. But I would sooner offend ten thousand sinners than offend God by being unfaithful.

Keep your tone loving but earnest, and if there is offense, so be it. You are talking to someone who is rushing headlong into hell because of a false hope fueled by their belief in a false god. They will never repent and trust the Savior as long as they cling to their idol.

Their offense is secondary to their fate.

The Cute Kitten

I was driving past a neighbor's house when he backed out of his driveway rather quickly. I slowed down to let him out, and as I did, I saw a small black kitten jump from the driveway onto the neighbor's lawn.

I watched it for a few seconds, and it suddenly dawned on me that the poor animal wasn't joyfully playing. It had been run over and was in its death throes. Finally, it rolled over and lay motionless. I was horrified and frantically followed the neighbor in my car to tell him what had happened. But he was driving too fast to catch. So I went back and knocked on the door of the house, but no one was home.

Later that morning, as I was telling my wife, Sue, about what I had seen, I broke down in tears. Earlier, I had been meditating on the necessity of having a compassionate heart. The book of Jude says, "Having compassion, making a difference . . . pulling them out of the fire" (vv. 22–23), and it grieved me that I would break down at the death of a little kitten yet have dry eyes when I pray for and plead with those who are heading for hell.

I'm not alone with my dry eyes and hard heart. That same morning, I had read the statistic that most of the contemporary church isn't even slightly involved in the task of evangelism. They're not going into all the world and preaching the gospel to every creature.

They've forgotten about hell.

That's easy to do when the function of the law is forgotten and God is just a nice sunrise. The laborers were few in New Testament times, and they are still few today. But this shouldn't be. What we profess to possess in Christ gives us a double obligation. We are morally obligated not only to tell dying sinners about Heaven but also to warn them about hell.

Although Jesus had a greater joy than His companions (see Heb. 1:9), Scripture says He was a man of sorrows, acquainted with grief (see Isa. 53:3). To walk in His steps and enter into the suffering of those around us is to walk a hard road. Empathy is painful and rocky, but we must walk in empathy if we want our prayers to be effectual and our preaching to be powerful. May God help us to rid ourselves of the self-deceiving curse of complacency sparked by idolatry.

Now Back to the Question

The question "What sort of God would threaten to torture people in hell forever just because they don't believe in Him?" is a *straw man*. In other words, the argument is framed in such a way that the skeptics can easily dismantle it and look as though they are the winners. God doesn't threaten anyone with torture. He warns them of coming judgment because He is rich in mercy. A question about hell is an opportunity to tell your listener about God's character. God is holy, just, and merciful. Sinners cannot stand before His goodness and live: "Therefore the ungodly shall not stand in the judgment, nor sinners in the congregation of the righteous. For the LORD knows the way of the righteous, but the way of the ungodly shall perish" (Ps. 1:5–6).

Neither does He warn sinners because they don't believe in Him. It's because they do believe and they remain in rebellion, because their deeds are evil and they love darkness rather than light. Scripture reminds us:

For all our days have passed away in Your wrath;
We finish our years like a sigh. . . .
Who knows the power of Your anger?
For as the fear of You, so is Your wrath.
So teach us to number our days,
That we may gain a heart of wisdom.
(Ps. 90:9, 11–12)

His warning to sinners is evidence of his love.

STUDY QUESTIONS

1. What was the crime of the three Northwest Airlines pilots?

2. Why would God's holiness consume us?

3. Why can we not look directly at the glory of the sun?

4. What must we never forget as we look at the Savior?

5. Describe Lady Justice.

6. Explain Romans 3:20 and Romans 7:7.

7. On a scale of one to ten, how concerned are you for the lost? Are you happy with that, and if not, how can you change it?

4. "Why should I care about what happens after I die if you can't even prove that there's life after death?"

Early in January 2018, all the giants of the modern technology world gathered together in Las Vegas for the Consumer Electronics Show. This was the world's biggest tech conference, drawing 184,000 attendees and 4,000 exhibitors. It was the showcase for man's amazing achievements. Unfortunately, rain hit a transformer, causing a power outage that left the brilliant minds in the dark for a long two hours.[1]

The entire world sits in the dark shadow of death. Humanity doesn't have a spark of light when it comes to the afterlife. And when you ask someone about the afterlife, "No one knows" is the answer they will so often give. For billions, death is the big mystery. They don't know why humanity as a whole is destined to die or what happens to our souls after we die. People who ask the current question are engaging with one of life's greatest mysteries, and they want to know what convinces you that there is an afterlife.

Of course, there are unbelievers to whom death is no mystery at all. They say, "There is no afterlife!" Some of them have no basis whatsoever for making such a claim. Others base their belief on the fact that there are no brain waves after someone dies. But the unbeliever who believes this has no brain waves before death. A dead person has no brain waves because they are dead. Their life—their soul—has passed on.

The "no one knows if there's an afterlife" crowd are also a little thoughtless. This is because the statement is absolute. They are claiming to know what every person on this massive planet knows and doesn't know. In other words, they are omniscient. In truth, the best they can say is that they don't know.

While most of the world is of the opinion that we cannot know if we have eternal life, the Bible says the opposite. It says that you can absolutely know, for certain, 100 percent:

> Whoever believes in the Son of God accepts this testimony. Whoever does not believe God has made him out to be a liar, because they have not believed the testimony God has given about his Son. And this is the testimony: God has given us eternal life, and this life is in his Son. Whoever has the Son has life; whoever does not have the Son of God does not have life.
>
> I write these things to you who believe in the name of the Son of God so that you may know that you have eternal life. (1 John 5:10–13 NIV)

Scripture couldn't be more clear: "that you may know that you have eternal life."

We can believe God's Word, or we can refuse to believe it. If we don't believe it, we call almighty God a liar. He has given us a light switch for the darkest of hours. If we refuse to turn on this light, we will be at the mercy of the king of terrors when the dark hour of death comes to us.

The Scriptures also tell us not to depart from the living God through "an evil heart of unbelief" (Heb. 3:12). The way to draw near to the living God is to trust Him, and the way to move away from Him is through lack of trust. If we have an evil heart of unbelief, we should repent of it as we would an adulterous or a murderous thought. The fruit of the believing child of God is joy and peace. That's what each of us can have right now through simple trust in the sure and steadfast promises of the God who cannot lie. Through that faith, we have a "living hope" (1 Pet. 1:3) in the living God, and we have that glorious hope because of the resurrection of Jesus of Nazareth.

Resurrection Proof

God resurrected at least three people from death in the Old Testament. He used Elijah to raise the son of the widow of Zarephath. He used Elisha in a similar way by raising the son of a Shunammite woman. He also resurrected a body that was tossed into a grave and touched Elisha's bones. But He raised a lot more. Hundreds of thousands, perhaps millions if you count the massive dead army that God showed Ezekiel. The prophet said, "So I prophesied as He commanded me, and breath came into them, and they lived, and stood upon their feet, an exceedingly great army" (Ezek. 37:9–10).

Then there were Lazarus and others in the New Testament, as well as the dead saints who were raised when Jesus died on the cross. The Bible says that as He died, "Jesus cried out again with a loud voice" (Matt. 27:50); perhaps the dead saints heard His loud voice and couldn't stay in the grave (vv. 51–52). In other words, it's no big deal for God to raise the dead. In Acts 26:8 Paul says to King Agrippa, "Why should it be thought incredible by you that God raises the dead?"

God raising dead people is not incredible. He made everything in the first place, and with Him nothing is impossible. Jesus said a similar thing. He told His disciples not to "marvel" that He was going to raise every dead person to life: "Do not marvel at this; for the hour is coming in which all who are in the graves will hear [God's] voice" (John 5:28). The impossible is normal with God.

However, the resurrection of Jesus from the dead was anything but normal. It was incredible, marvelous, and unique because of what it signified. It was more than a demonstration of the miraculous power of God; it was a confirmation of the approval of God. It was a statement that the redemption of lost sinners was indeed "finished" (John 19:30), as Jesus said it was when He was still on the cross. His resurrection permanently turned on the light in the darkness, and the darkness fled at the speed of light.

Charles Spurgeon said of the resurrection of Jesus:

> But it was more than a miracle of power, for all the attributes of God united their glory in the resurrection of Christ. God's love came there, and opened those closed eyes; His delight bejewelled those deadly wounds; His wisdom set in motion that pierced heart. Divine justice claimed His loosing from the grave, and mercy smiled as she lit up His face with an immortal smile. There and then did Jehovah make all His glory to pass before us, and He proclaimed the name of the Lord. If you ask where God's glory most is seen, I will not

point to creation, nor to providence, but to the raising of Jesus from the dead.[2]

Death still had power over all who had been previously raised by God from the dead. They still had to face its cold hand. But when Jesus rose, it was a permanent resurrection. He would never die again.

There are no words to express the significance of the empty tomb. Death could not hold Jesus. It was defused of its power. The plug was pulled. It was rendered useless: God raised him up, "having loosed the pains of death, because it was not possible that He should be held by it" (Acts 2:24).

The enemy was defeated, and the flag of victory was raised forever over the grave. Scripture tells us: "But if the Spirit of Him who raised Jesus from the dead dwells in you, He who raised Christ from the dead will also give life to your mortal bodies through His Spirit who dwells in you" (Rom. 8:11). His victory was our victory. We now say with Paul: "O Death, where is your sting? O [grave], where is your victory?" (1 Cor. 15:55). As Bill Gaither wrote, "Because he lives, I can face tomorrow; because he lives, all fear is gone."[3]

Look at this beautiful portion of Scripture:

But Mary stood outside by the tomb weeping, and as she wept she stooped down and looked into the tomb. And she saw two angels in white sitting, one at the head and the other at the feet, where the body of Jesus had lain. Then they said to her, "Woman, why are you weeping?"

She said to them, "Because they have taken away my Lord, and I do not know where they have laid Him."

Now when she had said this, she turned around and saw Jesus standing there, and did not know that it was Jesus.

Jesus said to her, "Woman, why are you weeping? Whom are you seeking?"

She, supposing Him to be the gardener, said to Him, "Sir, if You have carried Him away, tell me where You have laid Him, and I will take Him away."

Jesus said to her, "Mary!" (John 20:11–16)

Can you imagine the emotions that gripped Mary Magdalene in the garden tomb? Jesus had been dead for three long and dark days. But the despair that hung over her like a shroud left with one sound. It was Jesus saying a name—hers.

"Mary." Until that second, she thought He was the gardener. It was His voice, saying her name, that convinced her in an instant that He had conquered death.

Four-days dead, Lazarus too had heard His voice, and as with Mary, it was personal. It was his own name. "Lazarus!" The voice of the Savior saying his name raised him from the dead.

Marvel not at this, dear Christian, for the hour is coming when all who are in their graves will hear His voice. God knows you and me by name: "To him the doorkeeper opens, and the sheep hear his voice; and he calls his own sheep by name and leads them out" (John 10:3). What will we hear Him say at the resurrection? I wouldn't be surprised if it is personalized.

Still, the skeptic says, "That's just a blind faith. You can't prove there's life after death." Yes, we can. But like so much in life, the proof issues from living faith. For example, if you didn't believe in electricity because it is invisible, I would simply say to you, "Here's a fork; stick it in that live electrical socket." If you did that, you would experience its power flowing through your body. You would know that electricity is real.

Look now at these promises of God:

> *But you shall receive power when the Holy Spirit has come upon you;* and you shall be witnesses to Me in Jerusalem, and in all Judea and Samaria, and to the end of the earth. (Acts 1:8, emphasis added)

> For our gospel did not come to you in word only, *but also in power*, and in the Holy Spirit and in much assurance. (1 Thess. 1:5, emphasis added)

When someone becomes a Christian, they experience the power of God. They don't believe; they know. God gives them proof there is an afterlife the moment they personally experience the supernatural. Just like Mary.

Here is the gauntlet for those who stand back from the electrical socket and refuse to stick the fork in:

> Whoever has my commands and keeps them is the one who loves me. The one who loves me will be loved by my Father, and I too will love them *and show myself to them.* (John 14:21 NIV, emphasis added)

> *We know that we have passed from death to life,* because we love each other. Anyone who does not love remains in death. (1 John 3:14 NIV, emphasis added)

> Most assuredly, I say to you, who[ever] hears My word and believes in Him who sent Me has everlasting life, and shall not come into judgment, *but has passed from death into life.* (John 5:24, emphasis added)

To the skeptic who says, "Why should I care about what happens after I die if you can't even prove that there's life after death?" we say we can prove it. We prove it from the very mouth of the greatest of all authorities. This is not the mere word of a president or a king. This is the Word of the living God who cannot lie. There is no higher authority. Believe it with all your heart, and you will know. The Bible promises that whoever "believes in the Son of God has the witness in himself" (1 John 1:10). Stay in unbelief and you will stay in willful ignorance. And with that evil heart of unbelief will come darkness, death, fearful judgment, and terrifying damnation.

But if that is what the skeptic wants, it's his tragic choice.

STUDY QUESTIONS

1. Why is it flawed to say, "No one knows if there's an afterlife"?
2. Which Bible verse says that we can know we have eternal life?
3. How many people were resurrected in the Old Testament?
4. What does it reveal if we "marvel" at the thought that God could raise the dead?
5. Why was the resurrection of Jesus unique?
6. What's wrong with not believing God's Word?
7. What is an example we can use to show that faith can produce personal experience?

5. "How can you believe that God is love when there is so much suffering in the world?"

If you regularly stand on a soapbox and speak, you will soon learn that there's nothing new under the sun and that every question can be answered. This is because "I don't know" is an acceptable answer—and may be the only answer.

There are some things in the Bible—especially the violence in the Old Testament—that make me shudder. If someone wants to know why God sometimes sanctions violence, I have to answer, "I don't know." If someone asks why God put the tree of the knowledge of good and evil in the garden of Eden, knowing the horrific repercussions that would come, I have to answer, "I don't know." The pat answer—God didn't want to make Adam a robot—doesn't satisfy me, because in eternity we will not be robots. I'm sure we will have free will, yet it will not cause us to fall into sin. Why didn't God make our first parents as we will be throughout eternity? The answer is I don't know.

But the fact that I don't know doesn't bother me.

There are many things in this life I don't understand, and that doesn't bother me. I don't understand how GPS works, but I still use it. I don't understand how my sister in New

Zealand or my brother in Australia can FaceTime me from seven thousand miles away, but I still use it. We see each other's image and talk to each other at the speed of light without the use of wires. I would like to understand how it works, but it's not essential for me.

I'm content not to understand the ways of God because of what I do understand. I understand that God is loving, kind, and utterly faithful. All around me I see evidence of His wonderful creative hand. I also understand that He cannot do anything evil—not even slightly. So I trust Him, and authentic trust doesn't demand or need an explanation.

There was one day, however, in all my years of open-air preaching when my usual "I don't know" didn't cut the mustard.

I was speaking to a small crowd when an elderly man walked past. He stopped, listened for a moment, and looked at me with tears in his eyes. Then with anger, bitterness, and unspeakable pain, he wailed, "Why did God let my wife die so horribly of cancer?" I was dumbfounded, not only because of the man's emotions but also because he didn't want to stay for my answer. He stormed off, despite my pleas for him to remain.

Had he stayed, I would have tried to explain why so much suffering exists in this life. But my real dilemma would not have been why suffering exists but why God allows people to suffer when we see divine intervention so often in the Bible.

My other dilemma would have been the forum. The open air, with all its noise and distractions, would not have been appropriate. I would have liked to take the dear man to lunch and listen to his story before attempting to address the sensitive question of suffering. This is what I would have told him: every single one of us will taste some form of suffering in this life. People who ask our current question are often thinking about a specific time of suffering and wondering why God didn't prevent it. None of us escape suffering. We will all endure some combination of diseases, broken bones, toothaches, abuse, bullying, rejection, parental divorce, depression, loneliness, fear, and many other woes.

All the while, we enjoy the wonderful pleasures of food and friendship, travel, sport, love, and laughter. But the unwelcome monster of suffering pushes continually at the door, wanting to come in. If life were nothing but misery with no pleasure, most of us would be happy for the final curtain. But it's not. And that makes the final bow even more bitter.

Our question is this: Did God intend life as we know it? Is human suffering—the continual onslaught of cancer, hurricanes, tornadoes, floods, droughts, earthquakes, and death—all part of His master plan? If so, most of us would rather not be part of it. We can think of a better one. We don't want or need suffering.

The Bible says that we live in a fallen creation, one that came about because of the disobedience of Adam. When he sinned against God, he ushered in sin, disease, suffering, and death. When most Christians are asked what they want to do when they get to Heaven, they have a wonderfully spiritual answer. Mine isn't very spiritual. When I get to Heaven and see Adam, I want to smack him in the mouth for causing so much human suffering.

Boeing's Brilliance

Some use the existence of suffering to embrace atheism. Their question morphs into, "How could God possibly exist when we see so much suffering in the world?" But that is completely nonsensical.

Imagine you are sitting on a modern passenger jet. You relax in the comfortable seating, watch the personalized television screen with online access, note the amazing lighting and the cool-looking tray tables and armrests. Everything is designed for your comfort. You are in awe at how state of the art the entire plane looks, and you smile and whisper, "Boeing did an incredible job!"

Suddenly, the plane hits a massive air pocket and drops about four thousand feet. Bloodcurdling screams echo around the cabin and people are tossed about like rag dolls. As quickly as it began, the horror ends. Bodies of the dead and injured lie on the floor. Blood is splattered on the walls and roof. You hear the sickening sound of human suffering expressed with moaning and weeping. As you look at the scene, you whisper to yourself, "This is horrific! Therefore, nobody made this plane."

How could anybody come to such a conclusion? It doesn't make any sense. That's an absurd leap of logic. The logical conclusion is that something went wrong on the flight, not that nobody made the plane.

When we look at life's tragedies, it is illogical to say, "These things are terrible, therefore there is no maker." However, it makes perfect sense to conclude that something is radically wrong. And there is. The Bible gives the perfect explanation. Suffering should never be used as an excuse to reject God and His Word but should be seen as a very real reason to accept it.

When Adam sinned, he rejected God and took over the controls. We have inherited that sinful nature. All we like sheep have gone astray, and every one of us has turned to our own way (see Isa. 53:6). As the famous song says, "I did it my way,"[1] not as one who bows the knee in submission.

However, God has given His Word as a lamp to our feet and a light to our path. He's given us the Holy Spirit to guide us in for a safe landing. Being a Christian doesn't guarantee we will have a smooth flight, but it does guarantee we'll reach our eternal home safely. And that's what matters.

An Alternative Lie

There is an alternative lie to the foolishness of atheism. Some say that God is evil or incompetent. He knew that suffering and death would come as a result of sin, but He let it happen anyway.

There is, however, a huge problem in declaring God evil or incompetent. By blaming God for suffering, disease, and death, we bite the hand that feeds us. Everything we have comes from God. He gave us eyes to enjoy the beauty of nature, and He gave us ears to enjoy the wonder of music. He created taste buds to enjoy delicious food, and He gave us a brain, which hopefully we will never think of using to call almighty God evil or incompetent. If we call Him evil, we have no fear of God in our hearts, and the fear of God is the beginning of wisdom (see Prov. 9:10).

Anyone who fears God will always justify Him in the face of such arrogant and foolish accusations. God is without sin. He cannot do evil. He cannot lie or deceive or be incompetent. Everything He does is with the motive of absolute, pure righteousness. To assert the alternative is a dead-end street. It is to bite the gracious hand that feeds us.

Most would point to the book of Job as the greatest example of suffering in the Bible. In one sense, they would be right. It is about human suffering. Job lost his beloved children, his every security, his reputation, and his health. His wife told him to curse God and die. But he had a working brain and didn't want to bite the hand of God. He held out a long time before he began to even question His Creator and ask for a face-to-face meeting.

Job eventually got his meeting, but it didn't go the way he planned. God didn't answer his question. Instead, He asked seventy of His own, leaving Job dumbfounded. Job finally replied, "I have heard of You by the hearing of the ear, but now my eye sees You. Therefore I abhor myself, and repent in dust and ashes" (Job 42:5–6).

If you and I want an audience with God, we had better be prepared for a similar experience. Anyone drawing near to Him will become aware of their own sinfulness. The light shines so brightly that it reveals the darkness of our own heart. We would be wise, then, to say like Job that we have only heard of Him with our ears, and in our foolishness we have questioned His integrity. But once our eyes have seen His Holiness through the revelation of Scripture, we, like Job, will abhor ourselves for such wickedness and repent in dust and ashes.

The greatest suffering in the Bible, however, wasn't endured by Job. The greatest suffering any human being has endured was the suffering of Jesus of Nazareth. Yet, even in the terrible suffering of the cross, God was at work to will and to do His good pleasure. Out of the lion came something sweet (see Judges 14:14). Out of the darkness of the cross of Calvary came the glorious resurrection of the Son of God. God used death to destroy itself. It was hung by its own gallows.

When death tried to hold Jesus, He cut Himself free from its cords with the flaming sword of perfect righteousness. The Scriptures say that death could not hold Him. You could sooner contain the flaming sun in a thimble than death could hold Jesus in the grave. It was the dawning of a new morning after the darkest hour, and if the disciples had believed the Scriptures, they would not have been in despair during those dark three days.

Whatever cross you are carrying at the moment, dear Christian, no matter how dark the hour may seem, if you have repented of your sin and your trust is in Jesus Christ alone, faith will lift you up also. You can be sure that God is at work within you, all the while doing His good pleasure. You can be assured, according to the rock-solid promise of Romans 8:28, that all things are working together for good because you are called by God and you are working for His purpose.

The Man's Dear Wife

Now back to that poor man's wife who suffered through cancer. Why did God allow that to happen? My answer is I don't know. Was God punishing her for her sins? I know that if God treated me as my sins deserve, I would have been dead and damned many years ago. Why then did she get cancer and suffer so horribly?

In Luke 13, men came to Jesus and asked Him about the suffering involved in two contemporary tragedies. The first was an incident in which a huge tower fell and killed eighteen men. The second was when Pontius Pilate slaughtered some Galileans as they were making sacrifices to God. What did Jesus say about them? In verses 1–5 is the possibility of an answer from God in human form as to why those eighteen men and the Galileans suffered so horribly. Here is the short but pregnant passage:

> There were present at that season some who told Him about the Galileans whose blood Pilate had mingled with their sacrifices. And Jesus answered and said to them, "Do you suppose that these Galileans were worse sinners than all other Galileans, because they suffered such things? I tell you, no; but unless you repent you will all likewise perish. Or those eighteen on whom the tower in Siloam fell and killed them, do you think that they were worse sinners than all other[s] who dwelt in Jerusalem? I tell you, no; but unless you repent you will all likewise perish.

Jesus doesn't tell us why they suffered. It was His chance to solve this age-old mystery, and He chose not to address it. He did what God did with Job thousands of years ago. He left us hanging but with His faithful hand beneath us to catch us if we fall. Therefore, the only sensible thing to do in the midst of suffering is to lift ourselves out of the darkness of despair through trust in a faithful Creator and say with Job, "Though he slay me, yet will I trust in Him" (Job 13:15). And if that poor man who lost his precious wife would put trust in God into practice, he would have some oxygen in his suffocating suffering: "But I do not want you to be ignorant . . . concerning those who have fallen asleep, lest you sorrow as others who have no hope. For if we believe that Jesus died and rose again, even so God will bring with Him those who sleep in Jesus" (1 Thess. 4:13–14).

Because I trust in God and want the hope that He gives us, I'm content to trust God's character. When it comes to all the suffering in the world, I don't know what God is doing. But He does.

STUDY QUESTIONS

1. Why is it okay to say that we don't know the answer to every question?
2. What are some things you use even though you don't understand how they work?
3. How have you suffered? Be specific.
4. Did your suffering turn you away from God or draw you closer to Him?
5. Why is it illogical to turn to atheism because of the issue of suffering?
6. Why shouldn't we blame God for the suffering we see around us?
7. What is it that lifts us above the pains of this life?

6. "Isn't the God of the Old Testament different from the God of the New Testament?"

First, I'm going to address some issues that often arise when talking to a particular group of people who generally ask this question. More often than not, the people who ask it are atheists. Not always, but I've heard this question from the lips of more atheists than Christians or confused people with genuine questions. Know your audience before you answer.

Atheists are outraged by some things they read in the Bible, such as God telling Joshua to kill every man, woman, and child in battle. When atheists bring these kinds of stories up to me, I ask them if they really happened. They are adamant about it. "God commanded Joshua to commit genocide. And that," they say, "is morally wrong." But I have to remind them that God didn't do anything wrong, because, according to them, He doesn't exist.

Atheists getting angry about something they don't believe happened is like a person getting angry about Cinderella's coach turning back into a pumpkin at midnight. When it comes to arguing about what is right and what is wrong, atheists don't have a leg to stand on.

We know that God exists because of the order of nature, the existence of the inconceivable language of DNA, and the scientific impossibility of nothing creating everything. We know that He requires morality because of the presence of the conscience, and we know that we will be in big trouble on judgment day because of the condemnation of the Ten Commandments.

What we believe about right and wrong does matter. If we live by our own moral standard rather than God's, we may believe that dismembering a child in the womb for convenience is okay. We will appease the conscience by saying it's not a child. Our beliefs do matter.

Modern atheists have a creed that establishes their worldview. Their statement of faith, "I have no beliefs in any gods," is designed to confuse. It moves the goalposts out of sight, and the opposing team can't score any points. While atheists don't *trust* in Hindu gods, surely they have an intellectual belief that the religion of Hinduism has many gods. In fact, it is well known that Hinduism has millions of gods.[1] These gods are addressed by God Himself in the first two of the Ten Commandments. But more importantly, atheists are aware of the existence of the Creator, though they choose to deny it. We know this because, once again, God Himself says that He has given light to everyone, and that nature's design leaves all of us without excuse: "For since the creation of the world His invisible attributes are clearly seen, being understood by the things that are made, even His eternal power and Godhead, so that they are without excuse" (Rom. 1:20).

When professing atheists move the posts, we should move them back. The way to do this is to refuse to play by their rules. Their strategy is to use semantics to confuse, so don't even kick off until you establish your game plan. You need not argue about the existence of God, because you are dealing with offsprings of Adam. They have inherited a sinful nature and, like Adam, are simply running from God. Therefore, the Creator's existence isn't the issue. The issue is the atheist's sin. You want to show them that they're in terrible danger and desperately need the Savior. You won't be able to do that if you allow them to direct the conversation. Be bold and directive; lead the conversation immediately to their conscience.

If you stay with their intellect, they will argue with you, but if you speak to their conscience as Jesus did with His hearers, you will find that they are on your team. The wind will be behind your back. Ignore their semantics and ask, "Do you think you're a good person?" Then do what Jesus did, and take them through the Ten Commandments. If they allow you to do that, you've scored your points. Scripture says to be steadfast and unmovable, always abounding in the work of the Lord, because the energy that you are exerting is not in vain. You're not out to win the argument. Your goal is to win the sinner to the Savior.

Now let's talk about people who have a genuine question about God's character. Some people who ask if the God of the Old Testament is different from the God of the New Testament genuinely want to know if the God you believe in is consistent with Himself. The answer to the question is that He never changes. He is just as wrath-filled in the New Testament as He is in the Old. Those who believe that He's mean in the Old and nice in the New have never read the New Testament, especially the book of Revelation. What He is really angry about in both Testaments is sin:

For behold, the LORD comes out of His place
To punish the inhabitants of the earth for their
    iniquity;
The earth will also disclose her blood,
And will no more cover her slain. (Isa. 26:21)

It is a righteous thing with God . . . to give you who are troubled rest with us when the Lord Jesus is revealed from heaven with His mighty angels, in flaming fire taking vengeance on those who do not know God, and on those who do not obey the gospel of our Lord Jesus Christ. (2 Thess. 1:6–8)

The Amputees

Let's go back to people who just desire to confuse the argument. Another popular question atheists will ask to make God appear inconsistent and unbelievable is "Why doesn't God heal amputees?" This question concludes that there is no Creator, because God doesn't "heal" amputees. But an amputee isn't sick; he is missing a limb. But let's play this game just for a moment to see how childish it is.

The question is illegitimate. If I state that God doesn't heal amputees, I'm professing omniscience. I'm saying that I know historically what hasn't happened on earth up until the present day. I'm concluding that among eight billion people on the planet, there has never been a case of a limb miraculously growing on any human being, nor has it happened in the past. In reality, I have no idea what has happened to human bodies either presently or historically. In my limited sphere of knowledge, all I can say is that I've never heard of someone miraculously growing a limb after losing it.

Let's imagine that the inference of the question is correct—that God has never grown a limb on someone who lost an arm or a leg. The question then should be why hasn't He? He also may not have grown hair on bald heads, made short people tall, or made a third set of teeth for the toothless. Am I going to make a leap of logic and say that because I believe God didn't do these things He doesn't exist? Am I going to say that because I don't see new limbs, new hair, more height, or more teeth, therefore nothing created everything? Atheism has always been thoughtless, but the objections of modern atheism have taken it down to a whole new level.

More Atheist Favorites

Another common statement used to throw us off is that everyone is born an atheist. This implies that belief in the existence of God is indoctrination. But newborns are not born without intuitive knowledge. They know to drink and eat. They know to look you in the eye and respond to the human voice. They cry when they are unhappy and giggle when they feel delight. Babies are not born blank slates, waiting for someone to fill them in.

Faith too is an instinct and is not learned. Those same babies intuitively trust the hand that feeds and guides them. The statement that everyone is born an atheist isn't true.

God has given light to every man via the inner knowledge of the human conscience. It may take time for a child to comprehend that inner light, but it proves itself to be there. I didn't teach my children to feel the presence of guilt when they did wrong. Guilt came because of the existence of their

God-given conscience. Atheism, however, comes to some in time as they willfully quench the inner light. They don't like the feeling of guilt that comes with moral responsibility. Pretending that God doesn't exist is a temporary shadow in the heat of the desert.

The Glory of God

When the godly see massive rain clouds with glorious rays of the sun bursting through them, we can't help but think of the heavens declaring God's glory. But the "heavens" aren't confined merely to the clouds. They range from the air through which the eagle soars, to the flashes of fearful lightning, to the glorious majesty of the sun, to the breathtaking infinitude of space that can't contain Him. Our modern insight into these things has shown us that they are far more complex and wonderfully made than we have ever imagined.

Why, then, hasn't this modern knowledge brought this modern world to its knees in worship of the Creator? Could it be because paralleling the scientific knowledge is a massive advancement of our ability to sin? In the 1950s, if a man wanted to sin, pornography was underground and loose ladies weren't too easy to find. Nowadays, both are a dime a dozen.

Advertisements for what once were called whorehouses and brothels line the highways disguised as "Gentlemen's Clubs." The ugly scarecrow now wears a tuxedo. The instant internet feeds the insatiable appetite of sinful hearts with unending hardcore pornography and every kind of perversion.

The more that people are given to the darkness, the more they will hate the light, and those who hate God wouldn't give Him glory if you paid them in bars of pure gold for each uttered word. To give God praise is to crown Him Lord. That makes them morally subject to Him who said, "I am the LORD, I do not change" (Mal. 3:6). Even though the arguments of guilty sinners will change over time, we know that our God will never change.

STUDY QUESTIONS

1. Why should God be guiltless of genocide, or any other crime, in the eyes of atheism?
2. How do we know that God requires morality?
3. What is the statement "I have no beliefs in any gods" designed to do?
4. What does Romans 1:20 say of this world?
5. What is at the heart of the God issue for an atheist?
6. How do we know that the God of the Old Testament is the same as the God of the New Testament?
7. Why do you think modern knowledge hasn't caused this world to bow the knee to Jesus Christ?

7. "Would you sacrifice your child if God asked you to?"

This question reminds me of when religious leaders brought to Jesus a woman who was caught in the act of adultery (see John 8:2–11). The law called for her death, but Jesus preached love, mercy, and forgiveness. No doubt, they thought they had Him cornered. If He said the woman should be forgiven, then He was refusing to uphold the righteous demands of God's law. If He called for her to be stoned, then His message was not one of God's love and mercy. As far as they were concerned, He couldn't answer them without compromise. Jesus didn't say a word at first but wrote something in the sand. After He spoke, those who accused the woman of adultery began to leave, from the oldest to the youngest, "being convicted by their conscience" (v. 9).

People who ask you the current question think they have you cornered. It is a trap. If you answer no, then you love your child more than God. If you answer yes, then you prove to be some kind of psychopath and should be reported to the authorities. This is understandable in the light of stories like the following:

A father is in custody, accused of attempting to sacrifice his own son in a San Diego area cemetery. Joseph Ramirez, 30, took his family to Mount Hope Cemetery Saturday around 4:30 p.m. and told them his dead grandmother told him to sacrifice the 8-year-old boy, according to San Diego police. Officers released a report stating Ramirez had brought candles to the cemetery. One of the candles broke, and he used a piece of the broken glass to slash open his son's forearms. Ramirez then slashed his own forearms. . . . Once he's released, officers say Ramirez will be booked into county jail on charges of child abuse and assault with a deadly weapon. The boy was taken to Rady Children's Hospital for treatment.[1]

The provocation for this question is undoubtedly Abraham offering Isaac as a sacrifice because God told him to. What is the difference between Abraham and Joseph Ramirez? The biblical narrative begins with God telling Abraham to offer his only son as a sacrifice. On the way to the mountain, Isaac asks his father why there is no sacrifice to offer.

And Abraham said, "My son, God will provide for Himself the lamb for a burnt offering." So the two of them went together.

Then they came to the place of which God had told him. And Abraham built an altar there and placed the wood in order; and he bound Isaac his son and laid him on the altar, upon the wood. And Abraham stretched out his hand and took the knife to slay his son.

But the Angel of the Lord called to him from heaven and said, "Abraham, Abraham!"

So he said, "Here I am."

And He said, "Do not lay your hand on the lad, or do anything to him; for now I know that you fear God, since you have not withheld your son, your only son, from Me."

Then Abraham lifted his eyes and looked, and there behind him was a ram caught in a thicket by its horns. So Abraham went and took the ram, and offered it up for a burnt offering instead of his son. And Abraham called the name of the place, The-Lord-Will-Provide; as it is said to this day, "In the Mount of the Lord it shall be provided." (Gen. 22:8–14)

Let's dive into how this story is different from the story of Joseph Ramirez.

Isaac was Abraham's only son, and he offered him as a sacrificial lamb. A thousand years later, God would provide His own Lamb. Abraham was stopped from giving Isaac, but God the Father gave His only begotten son on the cross of Calvary. The incident with Abraham was prophetic of the man whom John the Baptist called "the Lamb of God."

Movies about sacrifice almost always have big box-office returns. This is because love is expressed in sacrifice. No greater love has someone than that they lay down the̶i̶r̶ ̶l̶i̶f̶e̶ for their friends. Love and sacrifice go hand in hand.

It's important to note that when the Hebrews were told to bring a sacrifice to God, it was to be a spotless lamb. No one was told to bring a diseased hyena or a rabid pit bull. A lamb speaks of pure innocence, and therefore to give up your lamb to God would be a heavy sacrifice. It was heartbreaking to give it over to such a bloody death.

When God asked Abraham to offer Isaac—his beloved and only son—as a sacrifice, He was asking him to give up what should have been his most precious possession. But it wasn't. Abraham's most precious possession was his relationship with the God who gave Isaac to him.

The incident is a display of Abraham's love for his Creator and a forecast of God's amazing love being expressed in Christ.

Abraham trusted God, and that trust expressed his love. He only did what he should have done. We are commanded to love God with all of our heart, mind, soul, and strength. He is the giver of life. He is the owner of our eyes, ears, blood, skin, hair, mind, heart, and soul. He created every atom of our being. We have these things only on loan. To love God in such a way is our reasonable service, and to give our love to anything above that love is inordinate affection. It is to love the gift more than the giver. Jesus said that our love for Him should be so great that our love for mother, father, children, and even our own life should seem like hatred compared to the love we have for the God who gave those loved ones to us: "If anyone comes to me and does not hate father and mother, wife and children, brothers and sisters—yes, even their own life—such a person cannot be my disciple" (Luke 14:26 NIV).

Abraham proved that he loved God more than he loved Isaac. He had the right order of affections. He was prepared to give his only son to the One who owned Abraham's only son. This took place not because God wanted to see what Abraham would do but because humanity needed godly instruction and a prophecy of what was to come—when our Creator would give up His beloved only-begotten Son. God gave up His perfect spotless Lamb as the ultimate display of sacrifice, and at the same time He revealed how much He loves us. "But God demonstrates His own love toward us, in that while we were still sinners, Christ died for us" (Rom. 5:8). His sacrifice is eternal evidence of His love.

There is, therefore, now no need for any other death sacrifice for our redemption. The only "sacrifice" God requires of you and me is to present our bodies as a living sacrifice, holy and acceptable to God, which is our reasonable service (see Rom. 12:1).

How to Answer the Question

If I heard a voice telling me to sacrifice one of my children, I would seek professional help. Mental hospitals are filled with people who hear voices telling them to do terrible things. The Bible says, "You shall not kill," and if you hear any voice telling you to violate the Sixth Commandment—from your mind or the mind of others—you are not hearing from God. It's coming from either your own sinful mind or from evil spiritual forces, and we are told to resist them, steadfast in the faith (see 1 Pet. 5:8–9; Eph. 6:12).

God owns not only our children but also every atom of the universe. But the world gives Him no rights at all. He is under a restraining order, and access to our children is quarantined like the plague. Like a dumb heathen idol, He is allowed only to sit in silence on a shelf in the home. He says nothing and demands nothing.

Look at how a young Oprah Winfrey found even one divine demand to be offensive:

> I took God out of the box because I grew up in the Baptist church and there were, you know, rules, and, you know, belief systems indoctrined. And I happened to be sitting in church in my late twenties. . . . And this great minister was preaching about how great God was and how omniscient

and omnipresent, and God is everything. And then he said, "And the Lord thy God is a jealous God." And I was, you know, caught up in the rapture of that moment until he said "jealous." And something struck me. I was . . . thinking God is all, God is omnipresent, God is—and God's also jealous? God is jealous of me? And something about that didn't feel right in my spirit. . . . And so that's when the search for something more than doctrine started to stir within me.[2]

For Oprah, God needed reshaping to conform to her own image of what He should be like. When you answer this question, make sure to tell your questioner the whole story of Abraham's sacrifice. Tell them that you, like Abraham, worship a God who is much bigger than your image of what He should be like. "Therefore, my beloved, flee from idolatry" (1 Cor. 10:14).

STUDY QUESTIONS

1. Why did the religious leaders think they had Jesus cornered?
2. Explain how the question of our sacrificing a child is designed to put us into a corner.
3. When Isaac asked Abraham where the sacrifice was, how did he answer?
4. Explain the typology of Abraham and Isaac.
5. What did John the Baptist call Jesus?
6. What is it called when we love anything more than we love God?
7. What can we learn from Oprah Winfrey's experience?

8. "Aren't religions the cause of more wars and suffering than anything else in history?"

Atheist George Carlin once said, "More people have been killed in the name of God than for any other reason."[1] It's taken by most, without question, that the famous standup comedian did his homework. People who want to see Christians as evildoers often bring up the subject of religious wars. Unfortunately for them, Carlin did not do good research. Fortunately for us, there is an objective source for those who wish to know the truth about the bloody history of humanity.

In their publication *Encyclopedia of Wars*, authors Charles Phillips and Alan Axelrod documented recorded warfare.[2] According to the encyclopedia, there were 1,763 wars up until 2004. Less than 7 percent were religious wars, and two-thirds of the 7 percent were in the name of Islam. So 93 percent of the wars in history have been more political in nature—for example, the First and Second World Wars, the Vietnam War, the Korean War, and others.

About 95 million human beings died in the secular First and Second World Wars.[3] But atheists have caused even more deaths and just in the last hundred years:

- Stalin was responsible for 60 million deaths; he was an atheist.
- Mao killed an estimated 40 million; he was an atheist.
- Pol Pot took the lives of 1.7 million; he was an atheist.
- Vladimir Lenin slaughtered 5 million; he was an atheist.

In a piece titled "Doesn't Religion Cause Most of the Conflict in the World?" atheist Jane Caro wrote:

> Indeed, while the religious have murdered throughout history in the name of their god, I've been unable to find any evidence of atheists killing anyone in the name of atheism. Atheists are no more or less capable of evil than anyone else, but it seems that murder, particularly mass murder and war, is a sin of commission. In other words, human beings are generally only prepared to fight and kill in the name of something. It can be a god, but it can also be a political philosophy—like nazism or communism. Many fight for patriotism: for country, tribe or race. Some kill because they're psychologically disturbed, but none—so far—in the name of atheism.[4]

But when the Reverend Jim Jones murdered 900 people, he did so as an atheist.[5] When Jeffrey Dahmer murdered and ate 17 young men, he did so as an atheist.[6] When communists slaughtered 110 million people, they did so as atheists.

Moral Relativism

The atheistic worldview has no fear of God and no binding objective moral standard. Atheism isn't a political platform; it's a worldview that denies the existence of God. Believing there is no God or not believing in any gods means that I can choose what's right and wrong. However, it is clear from Scripture that the issue for atheists isn't really about right and wrong. It's about their love for their own sins. People love darkness rather than light, and they have an arsenal of arguments to try to justify their sins. Believing there is no God gets rid of the problem of absolute morality (responsibility to God) and gives place to personal choice. I can choose to believe that abortion, adultery, pornography, same-sex relationships, fornication, and blasphemy are all morally acceptable.

If you are an atheist and you're asked if rape is wrong, you are forced to say that it is, because the alternative opens a can of worms. You would never seriously say that rape is okay. Just saying that could have your neighbors calling the police, because you would be a potential sexual predator.

But *why* is it wrong? The atheist's usual response is that it's wrong because it causes someone harm. That's the general atheistic criteria for morality. If something doesn't hurt someone, then atheists believe it is morally okay. If this is the case, there is a plausible scenario in which they would consider child pornography to be morally okay. A photographer offers them $75,000 cash to photograph their two toddlers without their clothes on. It will take no more than ten minutes, and the photographer will be behind a one-way mirror. The children won't be harmed, because they won't know about it. In fact, they will benefit, because the $75,000 will be set aside for their private education.

As an atheist, is this morally okay with you? No one is harmed. Be careful how you answer, because in 2017 a former USA Gymnastics and Michigan State University doctor received a sixty-year prison sentence just for having child pornography on his computer. US Federal law states:

> Images of child pornography are not protected under First Amendment rights, and are illegal contraband under federal law. Section 2256 of Title 18, United States Code, defines child pornography as any visual depiction of sexually explicit conduct involving a minor (someone under 18 years of age). Visual depictions include photographs, videos, digital or computer-generated images indistinguishable from an actual minor, and images created, adapted, or modified, but appear to depict an identifiable, actual minor. Undeveloped film, undeveloped videotape, and electronically stored data that can be converted into a visual image of child pornography are also deemed illegal visual depictions under federal law.
>
> Notably, the legal definition of sexually explicit conduct does not require that an image depict a child engaging in sexual activity. A picture of a naked child may constitute illegal child pornography if it is sufficiently sexually suggestive. Additionally, the age of consent for sexual activity in a given state is irrelevant; any depiction of a minor under 18 years of age engaging in sexually explicit conduct is illegal.[7]

If you publicly advocate child porn, even in the scenario described above, you may have the police on your doorstep quicker than fleas jump on the back of a mangy dog.

Atheism provides a moral buffet. It's a matter of picking and choosing what you like. But that doesn't always work with man's law and not at all with God's law. If in civil law I obey only what I like, I may or may not get caught. But if I treat God's law that way, I'm storing up wrath and will sure as "hell" get caught.

Origin of the Conscience

Another dilemma for the atheist is the origin of his conscience. Why does every sane human being have an intuitive knowledge of right and wrong? We instinctively possess this knowledge from our infancy. Some would disagree and say that right and wrong aren't intuitive but are taught by our parents.

Imagine a child is left without any moral instruction whatsoever. One day, he finds himself in court for multiple murders. Would he be taken seriously if his plea was "I didn't know that what I was doing was wrong, Your Honor"? Of course not. This is because of a principle in law known as mens rea, which is the standard common-law test of criminal liability. *Mens rea* translates as "guilty mind," and it signifies that "the act is not culpable unless the mind is guilty." In other words, where there is a conscience, there is guilt. And every sane person has a God-given conscience, leaving us all guilty of violating the moral law in the eyes of God.

Yet the voice of our conscience is rarely welcomed because we find pleasure in doing what is morally wrong. It is a heavy, wet blanket that falls onto the joy of sexual lust. But dulling the voice of conscience is about as intelligent as removing the batteries from our carbon monoxide detector because its alarm annoys us. A tender conscience will act like an impartial judge in the courtroom of our mind, accusing us of actions that violate the Ten Commandments. The first time we look at pornography, fornicate, commit adultery, lie or steal, or even kill, our conscience will call us out. The next time, its voice may speak with less volume. By the third time, it will merely whisper. When its voice is completely gone, we will find ourselves breathing the invisible poison of immorality unaware of our danger. The Bible calls such a state a "reprobate mind" (Rom. 1:28 KJV).

Can We Be Moral without God?

But there is more bad news for atheists. Can someone be moral without God? That can't be answered without a definition of *moral*. How high do I have to jump to qualify as a high jumper—a two-foot bar? The term *high jump* needs a definition of high, or it is senseless. There's nothing high about two feet, unless you're an ant.

What is the definition of *moral*? How high is the bar?

As we've seen, atheists don't have a definition. There is no objective moral standard. Morality is governed by personal perspective. The theistic world may have a high bar, but if it's not the same as God's standard, it is illegitimate. God's bar of morality is high. His standard is absolute perfection in thought, word, and deed. That means we are to love the God who gave us life with all our heart, mind, soul, and strength, and to love our neighbor (everyone else) as much as we love ourselves. That means we never lie to our neighbor, steal from him, hate him, gossip about him, or lust after his gorgeous wife. To sin even once in thought disqualifies us from God's standard.

In fact, morality can't even exist without God. Our eyes and ears, our brains, the air, the sun, the birds, and the atoms were created by Him. The emotion of love and morality itself would not exist without Him, because both love and morality are His very being. Scripture tells us, "Righteousness and justice are the foundation of Your throne" (Ps. 89:14). He showed us His standard through the law He gave to Moses. The full extent of what that law demands is seen in the Sermon on the Mount, where Jesus expanded the Ten Commandments to include *intent*. Among other things, He said, "You have heard that it was said to those of old, 'You shall not commit adultery.' But I say to you that whoever looks at a woman to lust for her has already committed adultery with her in his heart" (Matt. 5:27–28).

I have asked thousands of people if they think they are moral, and 99 percent believe they are. But in light of the Ten Commandments, it becomes clear that they think they are good because their standard of morality is very low. They consider themselves to be an Olympic high jumper when their feet don't even leave the ground.

The reason we are even looking at this subject is because we are moral creatures. We've been made with a yearning for justice. No other creature in nature sets up court systems and spends billions of dollars each year in search of equity. The biblical explanation for this is that man's Creator made him with a knowledge of right and wrong.

When Does Porn Become Moral?

Let's take a modern example to see how something evil can become moral in the mind of the atheist. Many now believe that pornography is not only moral but also natural. But not so with child pornography. We have already concluded that child pornography is wrong, but at what age does it cross the boundary from being immoral (child porn) to being moral (adult porn)? Is it when a child turns fifteen? Or would it become moral when she is a shapely eighteen-year-old? Could it be that personal pleasure is the influencing factor when it comes to judging when pornography becomes moral? The pleasure of the eyes crushes the conscience into silence. Eighteen years old—that's the age at which man's law backs off and allows you to have personal pornography on your computer.

The accusation behind the question that we've been considering in this chapter is that Christians are responsible for more evil deeds than any other group in history. Use the facts to set people straight, and then use the question to dive into the only basis for any kind of morality: belief in God.

1. How many people died in the secular wars of World War One and Two?
2. Of the 1,763 wars up until 2004, what percentage were religious?
3. Atheism has been responsible for slaughtering how many people?
4. What is subjective morality?
5. Name two moral dilemmas for the atheist.
6. Define mens rea.
7. How would you describe a reprobate mind?

9. "If God is so loving, why won't Christians let gay people be themselves?"

Christians have a public image problem. People who ask our current question and others like it are bringing up and perpetuating that image problem. We are seen by the world as narrow-minded and hateful people. We are painted with a broad and dirty brush, but we simply care where people spend eternity. Our bottom line is that we don't want gay individuals or adulterers, fornicators, liars, thieves, and many others to end up in hell.

And that is the key to inoffensively giving the gospel to an LGBTQ person: we do it the same way we share the gospel with an adulterer, fornicator, liar, or thief. Except, when it comes to the gay person, we keep in mind one more vital element. We don't mention the sin of same-sex unions until the person with whom we are speaking has a humble heart. This is not a compromise; it is rather a necessary discretion because of the mood of the society in which we live.

If I want to wake someone from a deep sleep because their house is on fire, I don't want to offend or confuse them. A flashlight in the eyes of someone in total darkness will do just that. If I want to bring them light, it would be wise to bring it with an urgent gentleness. The Bible says the servant of the Lord must not strive but be gentle to all (see 2 Tim. 2:24–25). That includes gay people.

First Timothy 1:8–10 tells us that God's law was made for sinful people, and it specifically includes those in same-sex relationships:

> Now we know [without any doubt] that the Law is good, if one uses it lawfully and appropriately, understanding the fact that law is not enacted for the righteous person [the one in right standing with God], but for lawless and rebellious people, for the ungodly and sinful, for the irreverent and profane, for those who kill their fathers or mothers, for murderers, for sexually immoral persons, *for homosexuals*, for kidnappers and slave traders, for liars, for perjurers— and for whatever else is contrary to sound doctrine. (AMP, emphasis added)

Let's talk about sharing the gospel with gay individuals. First, we should use the Ten Commandments to bring them to the knowledge of sin. Remember, they believe that the average Christian is hateful toward them. The use of the moral law is the way around that prejudice. You want to show them that you love them, and because you love them, you're concerned for their eternal welfare. You can do that if you do what the Bible teaches us to do—direct their conscience toward the law.

Gay people believe that Christians not only dislike them but also think they are all heading for hell. To them, hell is for Hitler, not for someone who loves someone of the same sex. Therefore, they usually have their boxing gloves up and are ready for a fight the moment you even hint that their lifestyle is unpleasing to God.

When I meet a person—for example, a young man—in a same-sex relationship, I ask him if he thinks he's a good person. When he predictably says he thinks he is, I take him through the Ten Commandments. Has he lied, stolen, or blasphemed God's name? When I ask about lust (see Matt. 5:27–28), I don't mention gender. After seeing his transgressions in the light of God's law, he will understand his guilt—and that he's headed for hell and desperately in need of the Savior. I don't mention his sexuality because I don't need to.

Before he saw his sin, he was proud and self-righteous, but now that he has put down his boxing gloves, he's clearly humble of heart. He is able to be reasoned with without being defensive. So I tell him that to be saved he must repent of all sin and trust alone in Jesus. I then show him what sin is by referring to 1 Corinthians 6:9–10, a passage that lists those who will not enter the kingdom of Heaven: "Do not be deceived. Neither fornicators, nor idolaters, nor adulterers, nor homosexuals, nor sodomites, nor thieves, nor covetous, nor drunkards, nor revilers, nor extortioners will inherit the kingdom of God." I gently tell him that if he has a problem with the list, he should take it up with God, because it's His list.

One of the most common ways to justify same-sex relationships is for someone to say they fought the desires for years and finally gave in when they realized they were born that way. That is similar to someone saying they always had a desire to commit adultery. They fought it for years but realized they had no choice—they were born that way. Of course they were born that way. They were born with a sinful nature. That's why they must be born again, whatever kind of sexual immorality they face.

God loves all people, and because of that love He wants them to be free from sin.

Cut Your Cloth

I had been asked to speak to about three hundred students at a Christian school's chapel and had been told that the subject was missions and evangelism. I planned to challenge the teenagers as to their evangelistic responsibility because of the existence of hell. It was a heavy word, so I had planned to precede it with "This is a very heavy word, but I trust that you will have the maturity to accept it."

When I arrived, I was horrified by what I saw. They were five-year-olds! There was no way I could share my prepared message. The host confirmed this by telling me to make sure I didn't speak above their heads. After an initial moment or so of panic, I cut my cloth to fit the situation. Those children, even at five years old, could understand that they should tell people about Jesus, and all went well.

We need to do the same thing when we share the gospel with others. We are speaking to those who are dead in their trespasses and sins. They don't have the spiritual understanding of even a five-year-old. We must use great plainness of speech and ask if what we are saying makes sense. If it has gone over their heads, we start again. It's funny when a church billboard says, "We love hurting people." But we can't be ambiguous when we are talking about someone's eternal destiny.

Jesus and Same-Sex Relationships

In an article titled "17 Things Jesus Christ Said about Homosexuality," the author listed the word *nothing* and synonyms for *nothing* seventeen times.[1] The seventeen-point point was that Jesus doesn't say anything about a same-sex union being a sin. Therefore, it must be morally acceptable.

Jesus was also silent about rape and kidnapping, but His silence doesn't mean these things are condoned by God. Yet Jesus did say that rape, kidnapping, and same-sex relationships are morally wrong, as summed up in His statement: "Do not think that I came to destroy the Law or the Prophets. I did not come to destroy but to fulfill" (Matt. 5:17). He upheld the entire teaching of the Old Testament moral law. Nothing was to be abolished or ignored, and God's law says that these things are sinful.

The moral law demands the death sentence for those in same-sex relationships; it also demands death for rapists, kidnappers, and adulterers (see Lev. 20:13; Exod. 21:16). That same merciless law waits for judgment day. The law will flash like lightning, and its fearful wrath will roll like thunder.

In 2017 a Peruvian crowd watched helplessly as a cow was caught in a fast-moving river during massive flooding. But the crowd became horrified when they spotted a poor woman who was also caught in the mudflow. Then something amazing happened. A huge container jammed against a bridge, temporarily holding back the mud and debris and allowing the woman (and the cow) to stagger to safety. After their rescue, the container was swept away by the mudflow.[2]

Ray Comfort

The entire human race is caught in a river that will sweep them into death and hell. But the mercy of God is like that container. It appeared in the person of Jesus Christ so that we would have a chance to escape the horror of impending death. But the time will come when God's patience runs out. That should give us a continual sense of urgency.

Most of the world thinks all is well between earth and Heaven, but we are merely in the eye of the hurricane. Outside of the eye of mercy, wrath reigns:

> O LORD God, to whom vengeance belongs—
> O God, to whom vengeance belongs, shine forth!
> Rise up, O Judge of the earth;
> Render punishment to the proud.
> LORD, how long will the wicked,
> How long will the wicked triumph?
> They utter speech, and speak insolent things;
> All the workers of iniquity boast in themselves.
> They break in pieces Your people, O LORD,
> And afflict Your heritage.
> They slay the widow and the stranger,
> And murder the fatherless.
> Yet they say, "The LORD does not see,
> Nor does the God of Jacob understand."
> Understand, you senseless among the people;
> And you fools, when will you be wise?
> He who planted the ear, shall He not hear?
> He who formed the eye, shall He not see?
>   (Ps. 94:1–9)

Our duty is not to let sinners—any of them—"be themselves" in their lives of sin. We must warn them of God's wrath.

1. How would you describe Christians' image problem when it comes to gay people?

2. Why shouldn't I use a flashlight in the eyes to awaken someone who is in a deep sleep?

3. What is the way around the prejudice of the average LGBTQ individual?

4. What is our objective when it comes to speaking with gays?

5. Memorize 1 Corinthians 6:9–10.

6. How did Jesus "talk" about same-sex relationships being sin?

7. What Bible passage says that the moral law was made for gay people?

10. "Are you saying that you are going to Heaven, but millions of sincere Muslims, Hindus, and Buddhists are going to hell because they don't believe as you do?"

Do you still beat up your mother? Answer yes or no. If you say yes, then you're beating your mother! If you say no, well, you've still said you have beaten her. You can't win.

This well-known question about world religions illustrates that sometimes we can't give a yes or no answer. No matter which way we go, we get ourselves in trouble. This is the case with our current question. People who ask this question often phrase it to make us look like narrow-minded, hateful, intolerant bigots.

To the average ungodly person, the existence of hell is unreasonable. No one could belong there except for Hitler and a handful of other evil people. This is because of their convictions when it comes to good and evil. They see nothing wrong with a few white lies, taking a little something that belongs to somebody else, and letting God's name slip through their lips in vain now and then. And, of course, there's nothing wrong with having a healthy appreciation for a pretty woman.

Before you answer the current question, take your questioner through God's law. This will show them that in the eyes of God, sin is exceedingly sinful. Because of His holiness, His wrath rests on every sinner, irrespective of their location on earth, their color, or their religious creed.

Now to the answer to the question: God will see to it that justice is done.

He will bring justice to the African tribe that has murdered an innocent man and eaten him. He will bring the same justice to the white man who has raped a woman, cut her throat, poured acid on her dead body, and gotten rid of it down the drain. God will make sure that such people are justly punished. His love of justice will not be confined or compromised. His omniscience and omnipotence mean that He will also punish adulterers, fornicators, and liars. Nothing is hidden from His morally perfect eyes, and nothing can stop Him from fulfilling His passion to see that justice is done.

Not every nation has the written law, but they do have it written upon their hearts. They have the headlines without the fine print. They are aware that sin exists, that they are guilty, and that Heaven frowns, and their conscience drives them to try to balance the scales. That's the foundation of their religion, something commonly called "works righteousness." They believe that their religious works will outweigh their sins on judgment day. They think they will be able to bribe the judge of the universe, and He will then duly dismiss their case. For them, Lady Justice will rip off the blindfold, withdraw her sword, and discard her scales.

They vainly hope to offer God the sacrifice of religious works in the belief that He will exchange them for everlasting life. Yet the Bible warns, "The sacrifice of the wicked is hateful and exceedingly offensive to the Lord" (Prov. 15:8 AMP). Isaiah 64:6 says of religious deeds:

> For we all have become like one who is [ceremonially] unclean [like a leper],
> And all our deeds of righteousness are like filthy rags;
> We all wither and decay like a leaf,
> And our wickedness [our sin, our injustice, our wrongdoing], like the wind, takes us away [carrying us far from God's favor, toward destruction]. (AMP).

If we offer a bribe to a good judge, it will only add to our crimes and will further bring his wrath upon us. How much more will an attempt to bribe almighty God to pervert justice produce greater wrath? We cannot purchase peace with God by any means. It is absolutely impossible.

> No one can redeem the life of another
>   or give to God a ransom for them—
> the ransom for a life is costly,
>   no payment is ever enough. (Ps. 49:7–8 NIV)

Our good news for guilty sinners is that God is rich in mercy and has provided a Savior to pay for their sins. His law was satisfied in Christ, and now God offers eternal salvation to every nation.

The gospel calls to Buddhists, Hindus, Muslims, religious churchgoers, and to atheists—whosoever will may come.

This is the greatest news that any of us could ever hope to hear. It is not a message of bigotry, condemnation, or hatred but one of incredible love and amazing mercy.

Listen to the Response

Listen closely to how questioners respond to your answer. If they are humble, they will be reasonable and admit that what you are saying makes sense. But proud, sin-loving atheists don't want a reasonable answer. They do not want to entertain the thought that sin is a reality and that hell exists. They will, therefore, be unreasonable. The truth threatens the many pleasures that sin gives them. If their question is insincere and you give them light, they will simply creep back into the darkness of willful ignorance.

Hypocrisy isn't confined to the religious. Secular hypocrisy often manifests itself in questions about other religions or about God's moral character. God is evil, they say, in allowing starving children to die. They don't care about starving children. Rather, they care only about trying to find dirt on the judge of all so that He has no right to pass sentence. Therefore, be ready for a proud person to respond to your answer with something disguised as tolerance and respect: "Whatever the case, I think you should respect what other people believe and not go around telling them that they are heading for hell just because they don't believe as you do." In other words, everyone should respect everyone else's beliefs except for yours. You should let them have their beliefs, but you can't have yours.

Agnostic versus Atheist

Let's talk a little more about your questioner. Maybe they identify themselves as agnostic or atheist. There was a time when those two words had different meanings. An atheist was a person who didn't believe that God existed, and an agnostic was a person who didn't know if God existed. But the two have become conveniently synonymous in contemporary atheist circles so that an atheist may legitimately claim both. The purpose of this illegitimate marriage of words is to cloud the issue and at the same time make the professing atheist seem reasonable. He is open-minded. Thus a new creature has evolved over time known as an *agnostic atheist*:

> Agnostic atheism is a philosophical position that encompasses both atheism and agnosticism. Agnostic atheists are atheistic because they do not hold a belief in the existence of any deity and agnostic because they claim that the existence of a deity is either unknowable in principle or currently unknown in fact.[1]

The goalposts have been moved in the fog of illegitimate definitions. Let's, therefore, put the goalposts back with the etymology and meaning of each word:

> *Agnostic* first appeared in 1869 (possibly coined by the English biologist Thomas Henry Huxley), and was formed from the Greek *agnōstos* (meaning "unknown, unknowable"). *Atheist* came to English from the French *athéisme*. Although both words share a prefix (which is probably the source of much of the confusion) the main body of each word is quite different. *Agnostic* shares part of its history with words such as *prognosticate* and *prognosis*, words

which have something to do with knowledge or knowing something. *Atheist* shares roots with words such as *theology* and *theism*, which generally have something to do with God.[2]

An agnostic is someone who doesn't know if God exists. An atheist goes further down the road to foolishness and believes that there is no God. If you are still confused, look to the Scriptures for clarity. God saw fit to put the definition of the atheist in the book of Psalms twice, perhaps because most of us are a little slow on the uptake. The biblical definition of an atheist is a "fool" (Pss. 14:1; 53:1). If we are speaking with an atheist, we are not speaking with an intellectual. We are speaking with a fool who has no basis for morality. He will try to justify the insanity of believing the impossibility that nothing created everything. Nothing can't create anything, let alone everything. Atheism is the epitome of stupidity.

The best thing, therefore, is not to play his foolish game. Don't get caught up in chasing what is designed to bring confusion. If he tosses the atheist/agnostic ball to you, gently toss it back and ask him if he thinks he's a good person.

Maybe you'll even be able to use that momentum from your "good person" question to ask him if he thinks all Muslims, Buddhists, and Hindus in the world are good people too. Every person on earth, no matter what kind of religious practices they may have participated in, will face God's justice. Your responsibility is to make sure that the particular agnostic atheist you are talking to knows that he too will face God's justice.

1. Explain why some questions can't be answered with a yes or a no.

2. Why is it important to take someone through God's law before answering the current question?

3. Define omniscience and omnipotence.

4. What Bible verse says that the sacrifice of the wicked is offensive to God?

5. Why are religious works offensive to God?

6. For whom is the gospel good news?

7. What's the difference between an agnostic and an atheist?

Ray Comfort

11. "Why are there so many hypocrites in the church?"

I was driving through an intersection when I saw a car coming toward me. I calculated that I could safely turn left before it reached the intersection. But as I turned, it seemed that the driver saw my intention, deliberately sped up, and turned in the same direction.

I was still able to safely turn before he did, but he felt it necessary to humiliate me. The manner in which he honked his horn would have been appropriate if I'd run over a line of two hundred blind puppies that were legally crossing the road. He then swung his car next to mine as though we were on the homestretch at the Indianapolis 500. He wound down the passenger-side window, yelled at me with words that you wouldn't repeat to your dog, and with his free hand, let me know that I was number one. I gestured that I was sorry, but it was too late. His short fuse had exploded.

It has been said, "Scratch a saint, and you'll find a sinner." But scratch some sinners, and you may find that they would kill you if it wasn't for civil law's threat of punishment.

Temptation, tribulation, and persecution reveal what's under the Christian's skin. The Scriptures exhort us to examine ourselves and see if we are in the faith, and life's daily tests offer opportunities to do that. They reveal if we are walking in the flesh or in the Spirit. How do we react if a thoughtless driver turns in front of us?

Self-examination is essential for the Christian, because there are many who think they can serve both God and the devil. Hypocrisy is self-deceiving. It's like bad breath—easy to detect in others but difficult to detect in ourselves. Our hypocrisy is an offensive stumbling block to the unsaved. We should do everything we can to weed it out of the church.

When I speak with a professing Christian who is obviously leading a double life, I ask two questions. The first is "When did you last read your Bible?" It's often a matter of years since they opened the Scriptures. The second is "Do you think you're a good person?" They almost always do, and that's the root of their problem.

In this chapter, we will look at not only a major reason why there are so many hypocrites in the church and what to do about it but also how to respond to those who stumble due to the many hypocrites within the church.

The Pursuit of Happiness

I'm sure Thomas Jefferson carefully chose his words when he said that one of the inalienable rights given to us by our Creator is the pursuit of happiness. Happiness is something we chase. We lust after the latest model of luxury cars, we seek a lifetime mate to marry, or we meticulously save up that first thousand dollars in the bank. Cruise ships, theme parks, and television advertisers hold up happiness as a God-given right.

Each week our ministry asks for prayer requests. One day I thought I would add a little humor to the list. I asked for prayer for Sue and me, because we were going to rough it with a day at Disneyland. I said that for my birthday somebody had kindly given us tickets. That somebody was Allen, our general manager. Disneyland was just twenty minutes from our home, but we hadn't been there for about twenty years.

Allen had sent us a list he had found of all the Disney dos and don'ts. Among other things it said something to the effect of "Don't even think about going on a Friday or a Thursday, or Saturday, or Sunday, or Monday, or a Wednesday." Those were the busy days. So Tuesday it was, which coincidentally was the day of my sixty-eighth birthday. This was going to be a double blessing.

As it turned out, there is no such thing as a perfect day to go to Disneyland. The predictable California weather gave way to wind, and we didn't bring jackets. Traffic and parking provided their own challenges. We spent more time on the freeway and in the parking lot than we did on the rides. Crowds were everywhere, and customer service was less than perfect. Yes, Sue and I still had a good time. But amid the chaos, we didn't find "happiness." We wouldn't have been happy at all if we were not already adept at being happy with each other.

Perhaps one of the greatest errors we can make is to think that happiness in this life is our chief end. We can gain it from sin (see Heb. 11:35), but as Christians we must ask if what we want to do is right, not if it will make us happy. Many "Christians" sit in church every Sunday only because they think it will make them happy. Of course, these people turn out to be hypocrites. They're going to church for exactly the wrong reason.

David's Pursuit of Hypocrisy

Let's talk about what happened when David, the man after God's own heart, decided to seek happiness. His pursuit of happiness led undeniably to his hypocrisy.

When Nathan the prophet approached David about his sin, he didn't speak to the king of a better life, with the promise of a wonderful plan that would give him true happiness. Nor did he say, "David, you have a God-shaped hole in your heart." The king had committed adultery with Bathsheba and then had her husband murdered; these types of responses would have been inappropriate, to say the least. Instead, the prophet faithfully spoke about sin, righteousness, and judgment.

Neither did Jesus nor the apostles speak about holes in hearts, wonderful plans, or human happiness. And neither should we when we are surrounded by those who have given themselves to blasphemy, adultery, fornication, pornography, lying, theft, and every other sin in the Bible. Jesus said, "Blessed are those who hunger and thirst for righteousness" (Matt. 5:6). Notice that he didn't say "those who hunger and thirst for happiness," because righteousness is the way to everlasting life—not happiness. That's what He preached in the great congregation (see Ps. 40:9). That's what the disciples preached. That's what the apostle Paul preached to Felix the governor, and Felix trembled. But few tremble at the sound of the modern, watered-down "happiness" gospel, and its converts are like the gospel they hear. Instead of responding to a call to righteousness, modern converts respond to a call to find happiness, and it's not long until many become disillusioned by life's trials and leave the church. Some, however, stay within its walls because of the social club benefits, mistakenly thinking they can have the best of both worlds—serving God and the devil. But their hypocrisy doesn't fool the world, and neither will it fool God on judgment day.

This question invariably arises: Why does God leave the hypocrite in the church? The answer is sometimes He does, and sometimes He doesn't. In the book of Acts, He killed Ananias and Sapphira for their hypocrisy. Others are mercifully left within the church in the hope that they will be awakened and genuinely repent. Whatever the case, according to Jesus, those who point a finger at the hypocrite will be judged by the same standard by which they judge others (see Matt. 7:2). None of us are without sin. Instead of being concerned about somebody else's sin, we should be concerned about our own. On judgment day, every one of us will give an account of ourselves, not others.

And that's what we need to tell those who complain about hypocrisy. It's not other people's hypocrisy they need to be concerned about—it's their own.

STUDY QUESTIONS

1. Explain the adage "Scratch a saint, and you'll find a sinner."
2. Name three things that reveal what's under our skin.

Ray Comfort

3. According to Thomas Jefferson, what is one of the inalienable rights given to Americans by our Creator?
4. What is perhaps one of the greatest errors made by human beings in regard to our pursuits?
5. What is more important than happiness for a Christian?
6. What is it that the Bible says delivers from death?
7. How did Felix the governor react to Paul's preaching?

12. "Why should we believe the biblical account of creation when evolution, which is proven science, says something different?"

When it comes to the question of evolution, I have to start my answer by talking about eyebrows. I can't help but notice that some atheists don't pluck their eyebrows. I wouldn't mention it, but when I go eyeball to eyeball with them, it's hard not to see the forest for the trees. My conclusion is that their beliefs must dictate how they face the world. In the genderless world so many of them advocate, surely they don't think that eyebrow plucking is only for the fairer sex. I suspect that perhaps the wild and bushy takeover is part of the evolutionary process of the survival of the fittest. At the risk of sounding petty and vain, when I notice personal haywire, I'm horrified. I pull it out like I would an ugly garden weed.

Psychology Today says that eyebrows are more than just a garden embankment to guide water and shampoo away from the eyes.

> Human faces are relatively flat. Alas, evolution has worn away the jutting jaw and the bulging brow ridge.

Fortunately, we still have one reliable landmark: the eyebrow. According to a study by MIT behavioral neuroscientist Javid Sadr and his colleagues, eyebrows have remained on our faces because they are crucial to facial identification. Faces without eyebrows are like land without landmarks.[1]

For the atheist who believes in Darwin's theory, evolution is behind the eyebrows. Therefore, we shouldn't interfere with the bushy landmarks. But I'm not a believer in the unproven and unscientific theory. If I hear a scraping sound on the doorposts as I go into my house, I take it that it's nature's way of telling me it's time to get out the lawnmower.

The atheist would disagree. Perhaps the ear hair outreach will in time evolve into wings. And that's not a stretch. With evolution, nothing is impossible. After all, it's responsible for our amazingly complex eyes and incredible thinking brains, so why not wings? According to that same *Psychology Today* article, there's even something going on if the garden is completely overrun by weeds: "Eyebrows sometimes meet each other halfway across the bridge of the nose, especially on men, to form a monobrow, which resembles the vanished browridge of our primate ancestors."[2]

Despite the evidence of the above-the-eye mustache, I don't believe that men are evolving beasts. I believe that although we are created in the image of God, we live in a fallen world in which nothing is perfect. Heads go bald, teeth fall out, skin gets wrinkly, eyes lose focus, the brain loses cells, bellies bulge, ears fail to hear, and eyebrows take over the face. And so most of us replace missing teeth, pull back the bulge, or wear contact lenses and hearing aids, because we want to retain function and personal dignity.

But for the godly, the ear hair and belly bulge issues go a little further than just self-respect. As a witness of Jesus Christ, I try to keep my lawn mowed and my weight controlled, not only for dignity or because of my vanity but also for my Christian witness. Many saved and unsaved individuals will not be impressed with what I have to say if I stand before them behind two dry tumbleweeds and with a built-in pulpit. My eyebrows would be a distraction. And so it is with people who ask about evolution: they are simply trying to distract you from presenting the gospel.

If you venture into the make-believe world of Darwinian evolution, remember that the devil is in the details. A great tactic of the enemy has been to confuse evolution with adaptation and speciation. Adaptation is some sort of improved function. Birds' beaks adapt over time. But they remain birds. Our skin adapts in the sunlight. Darwinian evolution is the theory that over time animals would change kinds: humankind (the human race), canine kind (the dog family), feline kind (the cat family), and so on.

There is speciation, or variations within kinds. For example, we have the huge Great Dane and the tiny Chihuahua, but both are from the canine kind. Within the cat family there is the domesticated cat and the tiger. Every kind has variation, but everything breeds within its kind and stays within its kind. No dogs mate with cats. Nothing changes kind or has ever changed kind as Darwin theorized. Ever. We see it neither in the existing creation nor in the history of the fossil record. There's nothing linking one kind to another kind. This is what scientists call "the Missing Link." Darwinian evolution is the missing "think." If you are interested in seeing a number of evolutionary professors from leading universities squirm as they try to think of scientific evidence for Darwin's fantasy, watch our movie *Evolution vs. God* on YouTube (https://youtu.be/U0u3-2CGOMQ).

The question, therefore, must be asked: If Darwinian evolution has no evidence or scientific basis, why is it embraced by so many? The answer is that wars are fought not only with guns but also with words.

On September 3, 1939, a ship was sunk by the Germans off the coast of Scotland.

> The first Allied casualties, and first criminal act of war, occurred tragically aboard a civilian ship. . . .
>
> The unarmed passenger liner SS Athenia destined for Canada had sailed from England on September 2. Nowhere near the size of ships like the Queen Mary, or Titanic, she nonetheless carried 1,103 passengers, including about 500 Jewish refugees, 469 Canadians, 311 Americans, 72 British, along with 315 crew. . . .
>
> On the evening of September 3, the German submarine U-30 was patrolling off the coast of Ireland.
>
> It spotted the SS Athenia at 16:40, and tracked the liner until 19:40 when the commander fired torpedoes, one of which hit the stern, fatally wounding the ship . . . presum[ing] it was either a troopship, a Q-ship (gunship disguised as a freighter) or an armed merchant ship.
>
> Ninety-eight passengers and 19 crew were killed. . . .
>
> Fifty-four were Canadian, 28 were American, raising concerns for Germany that the attack might bring the US into the war.

Hitler's propaganda machine was already in place. He ordered the criminal action be kept secret and adamantly denied the sinking of the ship, claiming the British had sunk her as "a propaganda ploy to bring America into the war."[3] Nations will lie to further their agenda, and twisting the truth is part of winning a war.

Atheists are at war with Christians. They fight to hold on to their freedom to sin, and our battle is to save them from the consequences of sin. We are confined to fight within the restrictive bounds of righteousness. They have no such boundaries. They are free to lie, and lie they certainly do—about God, the Bible, Christians, history, and evolution. Lying is kosher if it furthers their righteous cause. But this philosophy isn't confined to lying. It includes killing. In reference to famed atheist Richard Dawkins, *The Guardian* said:

> The British author made [a] comment in response to another user who said she would be faced with "a real ethical dilemma" if she became pregnant and learned that the baby would be born with [Down syndrome].
>
> Dawkins tweeted: "Abort it and try again. It would be immoral to bring it into the world if you have the choice."[4]

As a believer in evolution, which does not have an unchanging moral standard, Dawkins could have his own "honor killings" and justify them as being moral. That lack of moral standard—we are just animals—is also reflected in his curiosity about eating human flesh. He tweeted: "What if human meat is grown? Could we overcome our taboo against cannibalism? An interesting test case for consequentialist morality versus 'yuck reaction' absolutism."[5]

Absolutism is "the acceptance of or belief in absolute principles in political, philosophical, ethical, or theological matters."[6] Atheism has no absolute standard of ethics or principles, as evidenced by its historical trail of blood and terror.

If you debate about the theory of evolution, be ready to deal with fallacies that lead you down meandering rabbit trails. Believers in evolution, with eyes wide open, will present lies as facts and theories as evidence, twisting truth with more knots than you get in your garden hose. Don't be deceived when they try to present adaptation or speciation as proof of Darwinian evolution.

Instead, move from evolution to the gospel as quickly as you can, without being rude. Just say, "Let's get back to this later. I'd rather hear your thoughts on the afterlife. If Heaven exists, will you make it there? Are you a good person?" I can't emphasize this enough. We wrestle not against flesh and blood. The battle is against a subtle demonic realm that knows that the gospel is the power of God for salvation. The enemy wants you to stay away from what it is that saves sinners, and you will do just that as long as you argue about bones and theories. You want to lead the unsaved out of the darkness into the light, so take them by the hand and guide them. They are not your enemy. Your mission is not to conquer them.

We aren't out to win an argument about origins. Rather, we desire to win souls, and Scripture says if we do that, we are wise:

> The fruit of the righteous is a tree of life,
> And [the one] who wins souls is wise. (Prov. 11:30)

STUDY QUESTIONS

1. For what cause are atheists fighting?
2. For what cause do Christians battle?

3. What did Richard Dawkins say about a Down syndrome baby?

4. What is adaptation?

5. What is speciation?

6. What scientific evidence exists for Darwinian evolution?

7. What can you say to move the conversation to someone's conscience and, therefore, avoid arguments?

13. "The Bible was written by men. Don't men make mistakes?"

If Sue and I want to watch our favorite rugby team, we don't watch the game unless we know the outcome. Some fans would never do that because not knowing the outcome gives them a sense of excitement, but we feel differently. If we watch a delayed game and know that our team wins, we are able to view it without the slightest bit of stress. No matter how great the advancement of the opposing team, we know the outcome, and that's a great feeling. We can even smile when our team is down.

So it is with our Christian faith. We have inside information, and that knowledge gives us great peace. We know that we will win.

Jesus rebuked the religious leaders of His time, because they didn't know the signs of the times (see Matt. 16:2–3). The Bible is not only an account of the past; it also gives us an account of the future. Those who think it was written by men are woefully ignorant of the supernatural information it contains. But once again, our ultimate agenda isn't to convince an unbelieving world that the Scriptures are God-breathed. No one is solely converted by the Bible. We are converted by the power of God, and again, Scripture tells us that the gospel "is the power of God unto salvation" (Rom. 1:16 KJV).

When I was converted, the Bible gave me understanding as to what had happened to me. It didn't cause my conversion. That was a work of the Spirit of God, as is every new birth. Through the ages, many have come to Christ without ever seeing a Bible. This was obviously the case for much of early church history. For many years there was no such thing as the New Testament. It hadn't yet been compiled. There was also no such thing as the printing press, nor did everyone have the ability to read. The only "Bible" of which most were aware in the early years of Christianity was the Old Testament scrolls, and only a select few were allowed near them.

Early Christians were saved by the spoken gospel. They heard and believed that Christ died for their sins and rose again on the third day. Then, upon repentance and faith, God imputed His perfect righteousness to them, and they were made new creatures in Christ.

When I was first saved and felt completely new, the Scriptures told me that I had been born again. The "instruction book" gave me information. I had a peace that I couldn't understand. The Scriptures told me that it was the peace of God, which passes all understanding. I had a joy that I couldn't explain. The Bible said it was joy unspeakable, and it was the result of the faith that I had in the promises of God. I kept thinking about Jesus, something I had never done before. The Bible told me that the Holy Spirit pointed me to Jesus and exalted Him. God had opened the eyes of my understanding, taking me out of darkness and bringing me into His glorious light. He had saved me from the power of death and granted me the gift of everlasting life. The Scriptures explained this mysterious experience: I had been born of the Holy Spirit. The Word of God was a lamp to my feet and a light to my path, giving me comfort and sustenance.

When we are intent on convincing sinners that the Bible is the Word of God, the power of God—the convincing agent—is often neglected. Apologetics is a means to a glorious end. It fills in the valley and flattens the mountain—to make a straight path for the gospel that will bring people to Christ.

The apostle Paul said this of the message he preached: "And my speech and my preaching were not with persuasive words of human wisdom, but in demonstration of the Spirit and of power, *that your faith should not be in the wisdom of [others] but in the power of God*" (1 Cor. 2:4–5, emphasis added).

The Club

Skeptics say that the Bible was written by men and is therefore fallible. They want to discredit it, because it's a massive wet blanket that falls on everything they love. Discrediting the Scriptures is a hill they will die on. They are committed members of The Nitpickers' Club.

Jesus said of the religious leaders of His day that they were members of a similar club—The Gnat-Pickers Club. These unbelievers strained at the gnat and swallowed the camel. Nitpickers come up with things such as the Bible saying if you wear cotton and wool you will go to hell, we are to stone gay people, or a raped woman is forced to marry the rapist. These are actually straw men. For them, the ends justify any means. The ultimate end for these nitpickers is to dismantle the reality of hell. In order to do so they must discredit Scripture.

No matter what anyone believes about the Bible, it is God's Word, and the godly should approach it as such. It is full of mystery with precious gold nuggets of truth hidden in its soil. But skeptics have no inclination to dig for gold; all they see is dirt. Don't be like them. Dig for unseen gold, because if you don't dig you won't find it. God's word is a gold mine, and even Jesus spoke of searching the Scriptures (see John 5:39).

Take, for example, 2 Samuel 21:10. King David gave seven men to be executed, to appease an unjust incident that had occurred in the past. We don't know much about these men, but we are told about the reaction of one of their mothers: "Now Rizpah the daughter of Aiah took sackcloth and spread it for herself on the rock, from the beginning of harvest until the late rains poured on them from heaven. And she did not allow the birds of the air to rest on them by day nor the beasts of the field by night."

This is just a meaningless story to the dirt finder. He sees only a bloodthirsty king doing something that makes no sense and a grieving mother scaring away birds. But those who dig for gold beneath the soil understand that this woman did what the church should be doing. Her name means "hot coal," or a stone used in cooking. We are called "lively stones" (1 Pet. 2:5–9 KJV), who, clothed in the sackcloth of humility, rest upon the Rock of ages—Jesus Christ, the foundation of our faith. We should be imploring God to send the latter rain of revival upon the harvest. "Birds of the air" are often metaphoric of the demonic realm (see Luke 8:5, 12; Gen. 15:11; Deut. 28:26; Rev. 18:2), which we are to hold back through prayer.

Jesus said that the Old Testament was about Him. Jonah was swallowed by a great fish and then spit out onto the land, and Jesus was swallowed by death and then resurrected. Joseph was betrayed by his brothers and then exalted to the right hand of Pharaoh, and Jesus was betrayed by His brethren and then exalted to the right hand of God. Abraham offered his promised son, and God offered Jesus, His only-begotten Son. God hid Moses in the cleft of a rock to shelter him from wrath, and Jesus was the Rock of ages cleft for me to save me from wrath.

Those who look for dirt will find it. God gives the proud just enough soil to bury themselves.

Another Question

When I start giving evidence for the reliability of Scripture, skeptics will often ask, "Is there any amount of evidence that would change your views?" Another way to put this is to ask, "Is there a possibility that God doesn't exist?" The questioners insinuate that you are brainwashed and close-minded—not like atheists who are open to change. They will lecture you on how science works. It is open to new discoveries; it is the key to learning. You, of course, want to be seen as being open-minded and willing to learn, but once again there's a problem. The existence of God is not negotiable, unless you are a fool, according to God's Word. The question is as intelligent as asking, "Is there any evidence that would convince you that the earth doesn't exist?"

The fact that the Creator exists is axiomatic. Everything we see and can't see, from birds, flowers, trees, and seasons to wind, air, love, and laughter scream of the genius of God's creative hand.

When atheists ask me if there's a possibility God doesn't exist, I respond with a question of my own. Are they married? If so, I ask if there is any evidence that would change their mind about the existence of their wife? They always answer that there isn't, because there is no other option. This isn't because they are close-minded or antiscience but because they have a relationship with their wife. What sort of arrogance, then, would I have if I began offering evidence that he didn't know her? So it is with the Christian. We know the Lord. Jesus said, "This is eternal life, that they may know You . . . and Jesus Christ whom You have sent" (John 17:3). End of discussion.

The Question of Rape

When someone wants to discredit the Bible, they often look to Old Testament laws. It is common to hear skeptics say that the Bible says a woman has to marry her rapist.

The Scriptures also say to enjoy this life now while we have it, and not worry about eternity (see 1 Cor. 15:32). But here's the verse in context:

> I affirm, by the boasting in you which I have in Christ Jesus our Lord, I die daily. If, in the manner of men, I have fought with beasts at Ephesus, what advantage is it to me? If the dead do not rise, 'Let us eat and drink, for tomorrow we die!'

Do not be deceived: "Evil company corrupts good habits." Awake to righteousness, and do not sin; for some do not have the knowledge of God. I speak this to your shame. (1 Cor. 15:31–35)

In context, verse 32 is speaking of the futility of life if there is no resurrection from the dead. If that is the case, we are no different from this hopeless and hell-bound world. We may as well "eat and drink, for tomorrow we die." Understanding the context of any Bible verse is essential if we are seeking the truth. When people say, "The Bible says such and such," ask them for the reference, and then read it in context.

While the Bible doesn't say "Thou shalt not rape" in the Ten Commandments, rape is summed up in the essence of the moral law, which says to love your neighbor as yourself. Love does not rape. Hebrew law considered rape such a serious crime that rapists were to be put to death:

But if a man finds a betrothed young woman in the countryside, and the man forces her and lies with her, then only the man who lay with her shall die. But you shall do nothing to the young woman; there is in the young woman no sin deserving of death, for just as when a man rises against his neighbor and kills him, even so is this matter. For he found her in the countryside, and the betrothed young woman cried out, but there was no one to save her. (Deut. 22:25–27)

Yet some claim that the Bible says the victim of the rapist had to marry him. He wasn't to be punished but to be rewarded with the unwilling woman as his prize. Here are the verses used to justify that interpretation:

> If a man finds a young woman who is a virgin, who is not betrothed, *and he seizes her* and lies with her, and they are found out, then the man who lay with her shall give to the young woman's father fifty shekels of silver, and she shall be his wife because he has humbled her; he shall not be permitted to divorce her all his days. (Deut. 22:28-29, emphasis added)

Unbelievably (in the light of verse 25 saying that a rapist was to be put to death), a number of modern translations interpret "seizes her" as rape. The Hebrew word *tapas* means to "take hold of something," to grasp it in hand and (by application) to capture or seize something. In Genesis 4:21, it is used to "handle" (KJV) the flute. According to the law, if a man raped a woman, he was to be put to death, and a dead man can't marry the woman he raped. So Deuteronomy 22:28–29 *cannot* be speaking about rape. Scripture says if "they are found out," implying both were guilty. It obviously refers to consensual sex. It's similar to what we nowadays call a "shotgun" wedding. They had to get married.

God's Word is invaluable to the believer. But verses out of context can confuse the faithful and unfaithful alike. Sinners will do anything to discredit the Bible, because they don't want to live the way that it demands. But it's our job to tell them the truth. Remember that the victory belongs to Christ already, and we can be confident in that victory.

STUDY QUESTIONS

1. Why is it good to know that as Christians we win?
2. What does the Bible say is the "power of God unto salvation"?

3. How is the existence of God axiomatic?

4. Why did the apostle Paul not use persuasive words of human wisdom?

5. What does it mean to strain at the gnat and swallow a camel?

6. How should we approach Scripture?

7. How did Jesus define a believer (see John 17:3)?

14. "You can't prove God exists; even if you could, if everything needs a cause, what god made God?"

The legal definition of *proof* is "the conviction or persuasion of the mind of a judge or jury, by the exhibition of evidence, of the reality of a fact alleged: as, to prove, is to determine or persuade that a thing does or does not exist."[1]

Even if a man holds a smoking gun, has a body lying by his feet, and has a motive for murder, and eyewitnesses testify they saw the suspect fire the gun, an unreasonable or prejudicial jury may not be convinced that the evidence is indeed sufficient "proof." This may be because they secretly admire the defendant or believe the witnesses have been bribed and the defendant framed. People who ask our current question are trying to ignore all the evidence for God's existence; if they admitted God existed, they'd have to change their entire life.

There is ample proof for the existence of God, but we have a skeptical jury who loves their sins. The jury will have to be overwhelmed with evidence to a point of not being able to deny it. This sounds like a hard task, but we have three witnesses. First, we have the Holy Spirit, of whom Jesus said, "But when the Helper comes, whom I shall send to you from the Father, the Spirit of truth who proceeds from the Father, He will testify of Me" (John 15:26). Our ultimate aim is to testify of Jesus and His redemptive work on the cross. We have God's help with that. Second, we have access to the sinner's conscience: "Who show the work of the law written in their hearts, their conscience also bearing witness" (Rom. 2:15). And third, we are a witness of Christ: "But you shall receive power when the Holy Spirit has come upon you; and you shall be witnesses to Me in Jerusalem, and in all Judea and Samaria, and to the end of the earth" (Acts 1:8).

In addition to our witnesses, all we need is just a little knowledge of science and to be a listener who has some common sense. Let's first look at the question of God's origin. A way to prove that the universe had a beginning is to refer to the Second Law of Thermodynamics. It says that everything is running down: "This law is about inefficiency, degeneration and decay. It tells us all we do is inherently wasteful and that there are irreversible processes in the universe. It gives us an arrow for time and tells us that our universe has a[n] inescapably bleak, desolate fate."[2]

In other words, everything is degenerating. The universe is getting older and consequently is corrupting. If we were able to go ahead in time 100 billion years, everything we now see would have turned to dust—even the rocks and mountains. Subsequently, if the universe was eternal and didn't have a beginning, everything in it would have turned to dust trillions of years ago because of the Second Law of Thermodynamics. Therefore, the universe must have had a beginning.

The Bible says that God was the first cause that brought it into being "in the beginning" (Gen. 1:1). So the atheist will often say that if the universe had a beginning, God Himself must have had a beginning. He was created. They maintain that He could not be eternal because of the same law, and they will often mockingly say that God, therefore, was made by another god, who was made by another god, who was made by another god, going back eternally. In other words, they say that the existence of God is ridiculous.

That argument might have been credible if God hadn't revealed Himself throughout the whole of Scripture as being a Spirit. He is not a material being, just as our soul is not a material being. But mentioning the soul is often a problem with atheists too. They are quick to say that if something is invisible, they don't believe in it. However, every now and then you will find one who is reasonable. Years ago I interviewed a scientist at UCLA. He adamantly stated that he did not believe in the human soul. But when I told him that the word *soul* and the word *life* were synonymous in the Bible, he said, "I believe in the soul then." He made a complete reversal in his beliefs once he understood the meaning of the word.

Everyone has life within their body. It's what allows us to live and move and have our being. If the soul left, we would be dead. Our life is our soul, and God is the source and giver of that life.

If I look at a photo of myself when I was four years old, and compare it to a photo when I turned sixty-four, I look completely different. Yet I am the same person—the same soul—sixty years later. The only difference is that I am older and have gained knowledge and understanding. My body

Ray Comfort

grew old, but my soul did not, because it wasn't material. It's not subject to the Second Law of Thermodynamics.

Because God is a Spirit, He is not subject to aging and corruption. He is eternal and, therefore, doesn't need a first cause. He just is. That's why when Moses asked for His name, He told Moses "I AM." He didn't say, "I WAS," or "I WILL BE." He is "I AM." He is unchanging, self-existent, and eternal.

Almost-Convinced Eric

I was about to speak in a well-to-do church in Southern California on the epidemic of suicide in our nation. Right before I walked into the church, I noticed a young man sitting a few feet in front of the doors. He was nineteen years old, his name was Eric, he was an atheist, and he wasn't going into the meeting because he had been dragged there by his parents.

I sat down and told him that an atheist is someone who believes the scientific impossibility that nothing created everything. Eric listened, and in time confided in me that he hated his stepfather, hated church, hated the music we could hear coming from inside, and hated his life. He had already attempted suicide and was considering it again. I spoke to him about how he wasn't a mere beast as evolution teaches, one tiny result of nothing exploding into everything.

I also shared about the complexity of DNA. For example, there was no way any person could believe that a book with coherent sentences, graphics, and sequentially ordered page numbers could make itself from nothing. It is outside of the realm of possibility. Scientists often call DNA a book because it is made up of coherent information. It contains complex instructions on how to make your blood, your bones, your skin, your brain, your hair, and your personality. Everything about you was in your DNA from the moment you were conceived. To say that a physical book made itself would be insane, and to say that DNA created itself is absolute insanity. The complexity of DNA is absolute scientific proof of intelligent design. To deny the existence of God is a denial of human reasoning, logic, and common sense.

I then took Eric through the Ten Commandments to show him that he was in big trouble with his Creator, which included the sin of ingratitude. It took time, but I could feel the hard soil of Eric's heart soften as we spoke. He needed to understand the gospel—that is where sinners see their value to God. It is in the cross we see His love toward us displayed in that while we were yet sinners, Christ died for us. While we are not worthy of salvation, we are of great value to God. The evidence was demonstrated on that terrible day two thousand years ago.

The way I spoke to him was based on my conviction, which is based on Scripture, that no one truly believes God doesn't exist. God's Word says that every human being knows of God's existence, as we saw earlier in Romans 1:20.

I spent about thirty minutes pleading with Eric and hated to leave him, but I had to get inside. I gave him some literature and left him in the hands of God.

The Root of Atheism

In the 1970s, I was sharing the gospel with a small crowd when something caught my eye. A group of people were following members of the cast of the famous rock musical *Jesus Christ Superstar*. They had come to the heart of our city to promote the show.

They entered the crowd I was speaking to, and it swelled to about one hundred people. I kept preaching, and to my delight and surprise I was heckled by Pontius Pilate and Caiaphas, the high priest. Both were dressed in full garb, and both had great oratory skills. Caiaphas, dressed in black complete with his phylactery, was holding a staff and saying things like, "We rubbed you guys out two thousand years ago, and you're still going!" During my preaching, the cast of the musical would suddenly burst into a harmonized, "Jesus Christ, Jesus Christ, who are you, what have you sacrificed?" It was surreal, but it was the perfect springboard for the gospel.

After I finished preaching, part of the cast packed around me and asked if I would come to the performance. I said that I wouldn't. The story is told from the eyes of Judas and portrays Jesus as a mere man. They asked again. I was adamant, "Thank you, but no. There is no way I would go!" Then they said, "We will give you two free tickets."

I took my sister, and we were kindly invited to meet the cast after the show. I told them that I thoroughly enjoyed it and even felt proud of them. Then I said, "But the Jesus you are portraying is not the Jesus of the Bible."

To which Mary Magdalene replied, "But we're making Jesus acceptable to the twentieth century."

And there is the root of the greatest sin of humanity. It's called "idolatry," and it's so serious that God saw fit to address it in the first two of the Ten Commandments.

Changing the nature of God in order to make Him acceptable to others opens the door to every sin in the "Book."

Hitler created his own image of Jesus and then used religion to slaughter eleven million people. When we create a god in our own image, we predictably shape him to conform to our sins. This is why you will hear someone say they believe in God and almost in the same breath say that it is a woman's right to choose the death of her unborn child. That god doesn't mind murder.

Idolatry also opens the door to adultery, rape, same-sex relationships, and even atheism. Atheists have their own image of what they think God is like, and He is nothing like what they imagine Him to be. The god that atheists don't believe in doesn't exist. It's a figment of their imagination—the place of imagery.

If we had a true biblical perspective of God, we would tremble. We would never embrace a lustful thought, let alone adultery. We would run from sin in fear, because "by the fear of the LORD one departs from evil" (Prov. 16:6). If we don't depart from evil, we don't fear the Lord; if we don't fear the Lord, we are snuggling up to an idol—an erroneous image of God.

Of course, people may never have the impetus to change their life unless someone witnesses to them. I want to give you some different impressions of the witnessing experience—from people who do and don't take the chance to share their faith.

Panic in Paradise

On January 13, 2018, an alarm was sent out informing millions of people in Hawaii that a ballistic missile was heading their way. The Laid-Back State went into a state of panic. Horrible though it was, the incident may have been a blessing in disguise. Millions of people were suddenly confronted with their own mortality because someone pushed the wrong button. For thirty-eight terrifying minutes, they thought they were going to die—until it proved to be a false alarm. The fact remains, however, they are going to die. One of the wisest things we can do in life is to consider the certainty of our death. I'm sure during those thirty-eight minutes many a prayer was uttered for the first time in a long time.

A woman left a challenging comment on my Facebook page. She said that people in Hawaii were terrified. But an even greater concern for her was that she hadn't shared the gospel with family and friends. She then pleaded for prayer and help to know how to share the gospel.

Red-Hot Witnessing Encounter

David Grantham is a personal friend who has been a Federal Law Enforcement Agent since 1998. He flies aircraft in counterdrug operations. When he told me that he shared the gospel with a well-known celebrity, I asked him to send me the details.

> While waiting for my order at McDonald's in Malibu, California (because that's all most of us can afford in Malibu), I noticed a tall fellow with a bright red ball cap and aviator's sunglasses walk in. Something about him looked familiar and as he removed his glasses I was certain I knew who it was. Being an 80s and 90s guy I recognized him as the drummer from a well-known band.

I sat down at a table and pondered my next move. A selfie, an autograph, do nothing? None of these are my style so it would have to be a gospel tract, and I had left my supply in my jacket pocket, which I had left in the car. I went and grabbed some million-dollar bills [tracts[3]], trying to recall if there were any with his band members on them (there weren't), and planned my approach.

He had sat down very close to where our small group was sitting. I casually walked up and said, "Hi, I really like your work."

He smiled and said, "Thanks a lot," very pleasantly.

I handed him a million-dollar bill and explained it was a gospel tract with a message on the back about Jesus. "It talks about what it takes to go to heaven. My friend here in Los Angeles has a ministry that produces them; it will give you something to think about." He nodded and began to look it over and thanked me for it.

I sat down at our table wondering how I could reengage without seeming like a goofball. Our group was having some lively conversation, oblivious to what was going through my mind or who I had been talking to. My mind was racing, and I heard nothing of the conversation going on around me.

After a few minutes, he looked my way and nodded cordially. That was all I needed. I walked back over to his table. "Hey, if you cash that thing, let me know; I have plenty more." He nodded and smiled again. I then talked to him in a respectful, conversational tone about the good person test, taking him through some of the Ten Commandments. We discussed the conscience, God's justice and mercy, why Jesus died on the cross, the born-again experience, and even how we do street preaching and witnessing.

He said he frequently goes to the Lakers games and sees those folks with all the signs. I assumed he was talking about

Ray Comfort

155

the turn or burn groups (which he was). I said, "It doesn't make any sense, does it?"

"No, it doesn't," he said. We then talked some more (mostly me) about God's justice and the day of judgment.

All told, I was able to talk with him for about ten or fifteen minutes. I even mentioned that I didn't want to hold him up if he had to leave. He didn't seem to be in any big hurry and was willing to give me the time to share the gospel. I asked if he had a Bible at home, and he did. So I encouraged him to start in the book of John and ask God to reveal the truth to him. As he left, he came over and shook my hand and thanked me again (he was among the most courteous, polite encounters I've had in a long time).

As I sat there, thinking about what had just taken place, I looked around the restaurant and noticed about a dozen other people who had not been inducted into the Rock & Roll Hall of Fame. They probably needed a gospel tract also.

So I stood up and gave every customer in the restaurant a million-dollar bill. They too were extremely polite and receptive.[4]

Bank Robbery

I was looking at our nearly finished studio, which had taken over a year to build, when Sue said there was a gentleman wanting permission to film in our area. I went into our store and met a man whose name was George. He was from Boston, living in Los Angeles, and his job was to secure neighborhood permission for filming. This was for an episode of a big-budget Warner Brothers television program. They wanted to block off the alley leading to our ministry. I was more than happy to accommodate him because I know (having produced a number of films myself) what a hassle it can be to secure permission from neighboring properties.

As George was filling out the necessary permits, I sat down and thought how great it would be if he sat down next to me so I could witness to him. He brought the completed form over to me and said, "Would you like to know the plot of the scene we'll be filming?" Then to my delight, he sat next to me and said, "It's going to be a fake bank robbery, to distract the police. Meanwhile, the bad guys are just down the street pulling off a much bigger robbery."

I showed some interest and then said, "George, do you think there's an afterlife?"

He responded by saying he didn't believe in Heaven or hell. "Heaven or hell is what you make for yourself in this life."

I said, "If there is a Heaven, are you going to make it? Are you a good person?" He was very open and listened as we went from the Ten Commandments to the cross, for which I thanked him. But when I offered him a book I had written, he said he wouldn't read it. George looked like he was born in the 1950s, so I told him that it was about the Beatles and said, "Take it out of courtesy, like we gave you a permit to film out of courtesy." He smiled as he looked at the cover of the book, *The Beatles, God, and the Bible*, and he told me he'd been there for the Beatles' first US concert. I signed the book, and when I gave it to him, he genuinely thanked me.

Don't balk at questions like "What god made God?" The questioner may intend it to be a distraction, but it's actually your way into a conversation. Find out why this person doesn't want to believe the abundant evidence for God's existence. Jesus used the subject of water to reach the thirsty woman at the well, and with a little thought we can sometimes find someone's interest in life that can encourage them to come a little closer to the light.

1. How would you describe the Second Law of Thermodynamics?
2. How does it reveal that the earth can't be eternal?
3. What is DNA?
4. Explain the similarity between a book and DNA.
5. How does DNA prove the existence of an intelligent designer?
6. What sin did God see fit to address in the first two of the Ten Commandments?
7. Define idolatry.

15. "Unbelievers are as good as any Christian, if not better, so why aren't we good enough to get into Heaven?"

One day I spotted two ladies and asked if I could interview them for our television program. As we talked, I asked if they were spiritual and if they would be comfortable talking about the things of God. That's when they told me they were witches.

During the interview, one of them said she was as good as any Christian. That statement is usually made when the person doesn't understand the nature of Christianity. Christians are not better than non-Christians; they are just better off. They are like two men in a plane, one who is wearing a parachute and one who is not. Both men have to jump. The man wearing the parachute isn't better than the other man, but he is certainly better off.

Christianity is not about being good. It's about wearing a parachute. The Bible says to "put on" the Lord Jesus Christ (Rom. 13:14). Those who trust in Him alone are saved from the power of death and from the horror of damnation in hell.

We don't live a good life to be saved, but we live a good life because we are saved.

An unsaved person could perfectly imitate everything a Christian does—from reading the Bible, to doing good works, to going to church—and would still end up in hell. Salvation isn't what you do; it's who you have. Scripture says, "Whoever has the Son has life; whoever does not have the Son of God does not have life" (1 John 5:12 NIV).

Perhaps you are wondering how to speak to modern witches. Or perhaps you are thinking the odds are pretty low that you would ever speak to one. That may have been true in past generations, but there is a growing interest in the subject. For some context, following is part of a witch's testimony:

> Once I was old enough to think for myself, I broke with the church on issues of sexuality, marriage, the right to choose and the concept of "sin." . . .
>
> Since the 1960s, the "pagan" movement—what most people are referring to when they talk about American witchcraft today—has grown into a hard-to-dismiss new religious movement. In this country alone, a responsible estimate places the number of self-identified witches (typically called pagan priests and priestesses) at about one million. . . .
>
> In the past, it may have been tempting to dismiss this community as Earth-loving crystal collectors or velvet-wearing goths. In fact, the dozens of esoteric but related traditions share a spiritual core: they are polytheistic, worship nature and hold that female and male forces have equal weight in the universe. Pagans believe that the divine can be found all around us and that we can communicate

regularly with the dead and the gods without a go-between. They don't believe in heaven or hell; many subscribe to some version of reincarnation, or a next world called the Summerland.[1]

Here now is the transcript of the entire conversation with the two witches I met (edited slightly for sense). Rather than name each witch "Witch 1" and "Witch 2," which may be confusing as to which one is "Witch 1" and which one is "Witch 2"—forcing you to switch from witch to witch, while not knowing which witch is which—I have ditched "witch" and simply called them "Lady 1" and "Lady 2."

Ray: Do you ladies think there's an afterlife?

Lady 2: Yes, I believe in the afterlife.

Ray: And what about you?

Lady 1: There are many afterlives. We just call it Summerland. It's kind of like you keep coming around until you've learned everything that you need to learn and then you can go to Summerland, which you would equate to Heaven.

Ray: Is this reincarnation?

Lady 2: Yes!

Lady 1: Oh yeah.

Ray: So what were you in the past life?

Lady 2: I don't . . . I don't know.

Ray: I've never met anybody who did know.

Lady 2: Oh no, there are people who have learned from their past lives. I've got a huge phobia about stuff around my neck. I don't like it, which will lead you to believe that either I was hung or beheaded or something like that. I've just never focused on really trying to figure out what it was.

Ray: Well, I've got a fear of heights, but it doesn't mean I was a skydiver in the last life and I lost my life skydiving.

Lady 2: How do you know?

Ray: Because I don't believe in reincarnation.

Lady 1: Wait a minute, I have a question. If you don't believe in reincarnation, then how do you believe that Jesus came out of that cave and resurrected?

Ray: Because that wasn't reincarnation. He said, "I'm going to raise my body from the dead. I've been dead for three days. I'm going to raise it up! No man's going to take my life from me. I lay it down and I have power to take it up." There's no man like Jesus. He was God in human form. I don't know if you know that.

Lady 1: He was a prophet; He wasn't God. He was a prophet who preached.

Lady 2: He was God's Son supposedly.

Ray: Well, the Bible says God was manifest in the flesh. "The Word became flesh and dwelt among us." The Creator became a human being with the specific purpose of dying on a cross. Now, do you think that you're a good person? If there's an afterlife, are you going to make it to Heaven?

Lady 1: Summerland, when it's my time to go.

Ray: What about you?

Lady 2: Yes, I'm very good. I'm in better shape than most Christians I know, unfortunately.

Ray: How many lies do you think you've told in your whole life?

Lady 2: Not that many.

Ray: Take a stab . . . ten? twenty? one hundred?

Lady 1: Counting your childhood?

Ray: Yes.

Lady 2: Everyone tells fibs.

Lady 1: (Laughter)

Ray: How many do you think you've told? And I'm not talking about fibs.

Lady 2: I don't know. I try not to keep track. I keep track of the good things I do.

Ray: So you've lost track?

Lady 2: No, I don't keep count.

Ray: So you have lied? Broken the Ninth Commandment?

Lady 2: Oh yes.

Ray: What about you?

Lady 1: Oh, probably dozens.

Ray: I appreciate your honesty.

Lady 1: That's completely realistic. Even as a child. Though things like "I had one cookie" or "No, Mom, I wasn't on the phone." You know, so how do you count that?

Ray: Have you ever taken something that belongs to somebody else, even if it's small, irrespective of its value, in your whole life?

Lady 1: No, I have not.

Ray: You've never stolen anything?

Lady 1: I have not stolen.

Ray: Both of you have never stolen a thing?

Lady 2: No, I don't want anybody to steal something from me.

Ray: Never downloaded music off the internet that's not yours?

Lady 2: Actually, no, I don't do that.

Ray: Never taken a ballpoint pen that belongs to somebody else?

Lady 1: Actually, yes, and I brought it back.

Ray: So you stole it and you brought it back? Why'd you bring it back?

Lady 1: Strict upbringing. Strict parenting. "Take it back. It's not yours."

Ray: Have you ever used God's name in vain?

Lady 1: Yes.

Ray: I heard you use it before.

Lady 1: Absolutely, because He's not my God.

Ray: What about you?

Lady 2: Of course, I do. But He's not my God.

Ray: It's called blasphemy when you take God's name in vain.

Lady 1: In your religion, it is.

Ray: Ignorance of the law is no excuse.

Lady 2: I'm not ignorant of Christian law. I don't believe in Christian law.

Ray: I know that. Now, Jesus said that if you look with lust, you commit adultery in the heart. Have you ever looked with lust?

Lady 2: Well, yes. That house we just drove by.

Lady 1: Have I ever what?

Lady 2: Looked with lust.

Lady 1: Oh yes!

Lady 2: (Laughs) That house we just drove by because I want it really bad.

Ray: Okay. I'm not talking about coveting. That's the Tenth Commandment.

Lady 2: You're missing our point. That's what you believe in. We don't believe in those.

Ray: I know that. That's why I'm talking to you. I talk to nonbelievers. So ladies, I'm not judging you, but you've both told me that you're liars, blasphemers, and adulterers at heart. So if you face God on judgment day and if He judges you by the Ten Commandments, do you think you'd be innocent or guilty?

Lady 2: Well, hold on. If He was a judge, I would say 90 percent of the people on this planet, based on the Ten Commandments, would all be going to a fiery brimstone.

Ray: That's exactly what the Bible says. It says, "Narrow is the gate and difficult is the way that leads to life and few there are that find it."

Lady 2:   Yes, we are born with sin.

Ray: That's right, and what about you?

Lady 1:   What? Then there's my question. If Jesus Christ, the Son of God died for our sins to wipe us clean and save our souls, then can't we walk around and do whatever we want, because technically, He's already taken the punishment?

Ray: That's true, but what you must do is repent and trust in Him. He died to take the punishment for the sin of the world. You and I broke God's law, the Ten Commandments. Even if we don't believe in the law, we still broke it. We violated it. We've got a conscience. We know right from wrong, and we're heading for hell. The Bible says that all liars will have their part in the lake of fire. And no thief, no adulterer, no fornicator, nor blasphemer will inherit God's kingdom. But even though we broke God's law, Jesus paid the fine. If you're in court and someone pays your fine, the judge can let you go and still be just. He can say, "This guy's guilty, but he's out of here because someone paid his fine." Well, you ladies know that Christ died on the cross for our sins. His last words were, "It is finished!" The debt has been paid.

Lady: 2:   Who heard Him say that?

Ray: Excuse me?

Lady 1:   Exactly, who heard Him say that?

Ray: We have a record of it in Scripture.

Lady 2:   But you know what? Nora Roberts writes a really good book so . . . let's just say, two thousand years from now someone finds a Nora Roberts book and thinks it's the Bible.

Ray: (Laughter.) Well, that's two thousand years from now. What am I supposed to say?

Lady 2: Exactly, that's my point.

Lady 1: I have one more question on that.

Lady 2: You're following a book that's super old, that was written, first off, three hundred years after Jesus died.

Ray: How do you know that? History Channel?

Lady 1: That's someone else's interpretation.

Lady 2: No, that's what they say.

Lady 1: What church do you go to?

Lady 2: And second, if you're going to start judging, pointing out that we're wrong, then the only true religion would be Judaism and Christianity.

Ray: You've got it.

Lady 2: And Catholicism.

Ray: Catholicism's different.

Lady 2: Oh, how is it different? It came much before anything else. Where do you think Lutheranism came from? It came from Catholics.

Ray: Luther was a Catholic.

Lady 2: And Methodists came from Lutheranism.

Ray: Luther was a Catholic priest who realized that eternal life comes as a free gift of God. It can't be earned, which is what the Catholic church says.

Lady 2: Exactly, exactly, you don't need to pay your price.

Ray: That's right. So you ladies already know, but let me just give a summation. Jesus defeated death and rose from the dead. If you repent and trust in Him, God will forgive every sin that you've ever committed and He will grant you everlasting life as a free gift. I wouldn't lie to you ladies.

Lady 1: That's not true.

Ray: It's the gospel truth.

Lady 1: Because of what it says in your Bible. Even if you talked me into it right now and said I'm saved, I have a tattoo. So I can't even become a born-again Christian, because I have a tattoo.

Ray: That's not true.

Lady 1: Yes, it is. It's in the Bible.

Ray: No, it's not.

Lady 2: Read the Bible.

Lady 1: It's in the Bible.

Ray: It doesn't say *tattoo*.

Lady 1: It's in the Bible. "Markings."

Lady 2: Do not mark your body.

Lady 1: You cannot mark on your body. It says that in the Bible.

Ray: Yes, it's Jewish law. Now listen—

Lady 1: I'm not Jewish.

Ray: I'm Jewish. God's not going to judge you for a tattoo. He's going to judge you for lying and stealing and fornication and blasphemy.

Lady 1: And how do you know that?

Ray: The Bible says, "Sin is transgression of the law."
        It's not having a tattoo. Sin is transgression of
        the moral law. And Ladies, I'm trying to say,
        God can let you live forever if you'll repent and
        trust Christ. I'm not saying, "Join a church."
        I don't want your money. I'm saying we're all
        pagans by nature. We make up our own gods. I
        was like that before I was a Christian. I made a
        god to suit myself and I snuggled up to my god,
        because he didn't have a moral dictate, didn't
        tell me right from wrong. But when I faced the
        God of the Bible, the God who created us, I real-
        ized I was in big trouble and I needed a Savior.
        And that's all I'm saying to you. We all need a
        Savior.

Lady 1: Just really quick. I want to go back to Hallow-
        een. Halloween is a horrible misconception, and
        pagans have got a terrible, bad rap because of
        it. To be honest, Halloween had nothing to do
        with any kind of religion. Not Christianity, not
        paganism. It had to do with poor children in the
        villages. When people would make their pies
        and sweet cakes, they set them on the windowsill
        to cool, and poor children would come by and
        steal them. So, they would put something over
        their head—now they call it a "costume"—to
        disguise themselves, so they wouldn't get caught
        and punished by the town or by their parents.
        Halloween morphed into a commercial holiday,
        but it had nothing to do with any religion.

Ray: Big money in it. Like everything else. Same with Christmas. So what were you going to say?

Lady 2: Like Valentine's Day, Easter, and Thanksgiving . . .

Ray: And Father's Day and Mother's Day. Please think about what we talked about. I'll think about what you said about paganism and witchcraft. But just think about your sins. Think about the Savior, what happened on that cross. Think about the fact that every day 150,000 people die—people just like you and me, people who love life—54 million every year. I'm saying God's given you a will to live; listen to it. Check it out. Jesus said, "I am the way, the truth, and the life. No one comes to the Father except through Me." And the Bible says He's abolished death. Jesus Christ has abolished death, and if that's true, you owe it to your good sense just to look into it.

Lady 1: You don't have to take our word for it. Knowledge is power. You have a little bit of knowledge about our beliefs, and we clearly have knowledge about yours, and so we've researched. All we ask is that when you go home and whatever it is that you look up, not the History Channel but whatever it is that you look up to research things, even scientifically, research it a little. That's all we ask. We're not saying, we're right and you're wrong. We hope that you're not saying vice versa, because in the end, everyone's allowed to believe in whatever god or higher being they believe in, as long as they're living a moral code.

Ray: Well, you and I aren't. We've broken those commandments. So we need a Savior. That's what I'm saying. If God gives you justice, you'll end up in hell. I'd hate that to happen to you. You're not good. You're like the rest of us.

Lady 2: I am, I am pretty good.

Ray: A morally good person?

Lady 2: Yes, I am.

Ray: Self-admitted liar and blasphemer and adulterer at heart? We've all sinned. We've broken those commandments, and we make the mistake of measuring ourselves by man's standards and not God's. God's going to judge us by His commandments, not ours.

Lady 2: Those are your commandments that you follow.

Ray: They're not my commandments. They're God's commandments.

Lady 2: But, He's not my God.

Ray: Thank you very much for talking to me. It's been very colorful. I've really enjoyed it, and I trust that you'll think about what we talked about today.

Lady 1: Thank you very much!

Lady 2: Have a good day.

I wanted to share this conversation so that you could see that evangelism can be messy. But in the end, it's all about bringing the conversation back to the gospel. That's all I did with the witches, and that's all that you have to do with the people you meet.

When people say that Christians aren't better than anyone else, what they're revealing is that they don't have an understanding of salvation. You need to tell them that salvation isn't what you do, it's who you place your trust in. That's what makes Christians different from all the other people in the world.

STUDY QUESTIONS

1. Would you feel comfortable talking to witches?
2. When reading the transcript, was there any time your heart raced a little? If so, why?
3. Did you notice any potential rabbit trails? If so, where?
4. Reference three Bible verses that say Jesus is God.
5. In a nutshell, what does the Catholic church say about salvation?
6. What is the biblical definition of sin?
7. What is success in an evangelism encounter of this nature?

16. "What happens to those who have never heard the gospel?"

As we have so often seen in Scripture, everyone knows that God exists because the heavens declare His glory. Each day and night speaks about Him. The invisible things of Him are clearly seen in the things that are made. They know of God, but they refuse to glorify Him as God. What, then, is the eternal fate of those who never hear the claims of the gospel? Surely, God has a moral obligation to reach them. It seems only fair.

To answer this question, let's go back to criminal court. Think of a guilty criminal who is waiting to be sentenced by a judge. This individual has committed very serious crimes. The fine is $1 million or six years in prison. If the judge shows any mercy, it is because of the judge's own prerogative. He owes the criminal nothing but justice.

As the judge of the universe, God is under no obligation to give us anything but justice. But because He is rich in mercy, He came down to the criminals and paid the fine so that His mercy could be extended.

The Bible is very clear that if a man or woman has violated any of the Ten Commandments, they will come under His just wrath on judgment day, despite their location on earth. If a Pygmy in Africa or an ignorant savage on Wall Street dies in their sins, they will end up in God's prison. Hell will be their terrible fate. Perfect justice will be done on that day, despite race, creed, or color, and the standard by which they will be judged will be the moral law (see Rom. 2:12; James 2:12).

Thank God that He has no pleasure in the death of the wicked. He is not willing that any perish. His will is that all come to repentance, and so He commands us to reach out to the lost with the message of mercy in Christ. God has no moral obligation to reach out to guilty sinners, but now, because of the offer of mercy, we are the ones with a moral obligation to reach out to them. If hopeless damnation was awaiting the lost, we could justify doing nothing because there would be nothing to give them. But because everlasting life is being offered to the hopeless, we must plead with them to turn to the Savior. To remain silent about Jesus is worse than standing by and letting a man drown when there is a rope lying at your feet.

At the risk of sounding petty, I once felt frustrated when I listened to a respected Bible teacher talk about how the early disciples preached "the Word." He said that they exalted the pulpit. In other words, the pulpit was a special place—a sanctified, holy place where the Word of God was expounded for God's people. That's true, but let me focus in on that a little. The early church preached the gospel. Yes, they also taught sound doctrine, but to leave out the emphasis they placed on the gospel is to neglect the reality that sinners are going to hell. It takes the focus off desperate evangelism. If the modern church needs to focus on anything, it is the fate of the unsaved. Paul spoke of being in debt to the lost: "I am a debtor both to Greeks and to barbarians, both to wise and to unwise. So, as much as is in me, I am ready to preach the gospel to you who are in Rome also" (Rom. 1:14–15).

The reality of hell is our motivation for asking missionaries to leave the safety and comfort of their homes and endure great hardship to reach the unsaved. But each missionary who takes the gospel to the unsaved knows that the real hardship was endured two thousand years ago. If we are really concerned about what happens to those who have never heard the gospel, we should get right with God ourselves, become missionaries at home or abroad, and go tell them that they can live forever.

Walk in My Shoes

A friend named Dan Arnold once gave me some boots as a gift. But he suddenly went to be with the Lord, and so they became very special to me. In honor of Dan, I determined to wear them every time I stood in a pulpit.

After Dan passed, I was asked by Ken Ham, president of Answers in Genesis, to play an important part in a movie that would be shown to the millions who visit his amazing Ark Encounter in Kentucky (https://arkencounter.com/).

They wanted to film me preaching to a very cynical secular film crew who were doing a story about the ark. This was going to be a big deal, probably the most important preaching event in which I would ever be involved.

The day of the filming, I gathered my clothes together. I had a number of backup shirts and various ties. This was too important to mess up with the wrong-colored clothing. I wore shorts and sneakers for the two-hour drive to the studio. But as I lined up my clothes to get ready to go on set, I noticed that I had forgotten one thing—my precious boots! I couldn't believe how dumb I'd been. I ended up borrowing my son-in-law's shoes, socks, and even his matching belt. He is an Arab and I am a Jew, so it was an experience to walk in his shoes.

Empathy walks in the shoes of both the Pygmy and the Wall Street tycoon. It feels their terror on judgment day. It makes us groan in prayer as we think of their fate and ask God what we can do to reach them. Charles Spurgeon said of prayer: "Live and die without prayer, and you will pray long enough when you get to Hell."[1]

You may be familiar with a famous sculpture called *The Thinker*. It shows a seated man thoughtfully leaning on his fist. This is often used to depict an intellectual. However, its origin shows that it has a much deeper meaning. It was a small part of a larger sculpture by French artist Auguste Rodin. The complete sculpture is based on a scene from *Inferno*, the first section of Dante Alighieri's *Divine Comedy*. The thinker is said to be Adam, looking down at those who are going into hell.[2]

Each of us should be deep in contemplative thought, daily meditating on those poor souls who are going to hell. But we should be doing more than merely sitting and thinking. They need to hear the gospel.

Coining a Phrase

One early morning as I was riding my bike, I saw someone walking along in front of me. As I passed him, I said warmly,

"Good morning!" He responded just as warmly, so I stopped and handed him one of our coins with the Ten Commandments on one side and the gospel on the other.[3]

His reaction was very positive, so we introduced ourselves and continued talking. His name was Chris, and I asked him if he was a Christian. He answered that he was a Catholic. He thought he was good enough to go to Heaven, but when we went through the commandments, he proved to be just like the rest of us—a lying thief, a blasphemer, and an adulterer at heart. But he then said that God was forgiving and that on judgment day he would be found innocent. I told him that God was forgiving, but He forgave on a condition. I said, "I think you may have forgotten why God can forgive. You're like a man who believes in a parachute and jumps without putting it on."

When I explained the gospel, Chris's eyes went wide with amazement. I asked, "Does this make sense to you?"

He responded by saying that what I had told him had given him a whole new perspective. He said, "I'm doing a 180 right now!"

I asked if I could pray with him, and as we prayed on the sidewalk, he removed his hat in respect. I thought that was great, but as I ended the prayer, I noticed he wobbled slightly. When we finished praying, I said, "Chris, have you been drinking?"

He replied, "Just a little bit last night."

My heart sank, and I asked if the alcohol had clouded his thoughts and hindered anything I had said to him. He was adamant that it hadn't and added that he had a Bible at home.

I would rather he had been stone-cold sober, but my consolation was that God is faithful to honor His Word, that our labors are never in vain (see 1 Cor. 15:58), and that if a legion of demons couldn't stop a demon-possessed sinner from coming to the feet of Jesus (see Mark 5:1–20; Luke 8:26–39), neither could the demon of alcohol stop this man.

An Important Sidenote about Addictions

I was in charge of the Drug Prevention Center in New Zealand for a number of years, and through it I did counseling for families whose kids were using illegal drugs. I found that it was very important (for those who are addicted to alcohol or drugs) to deal with the cause rather than the symptoms. There is a measure of sympathy for those in such a state and with it a temptation to offer the gospel as a means of overcoming addiction. But this is liable to produce a false conversion, because the sinner responds to having his alcohol problem fixed rather than having his sins forgiven. If we go that route, rather than first confronting the sinful nature through the use of God's law, we will wipe away the web and leave the spider. Addiction to alcohol and certain other drugs is overpowering. I liken it to the need that you and I have to swallow. We simply cannot stop; we are preprogrammed to swallow between six and eight hundred times each day, most often without even realizing it. Try not to swallow for a few moments, and feel the panic of a physical addiction.

That's why all sinners, both those addicted to alcohol and those addicted to sin, need to hear about the law and future punishment. Addiction is devastating at best, but if we are responsible for a false conversion, the later end truly becomes worse than the first. Don't be tempted in the name of love and compassion to yield to sympathizing with the symptoms but ignoring the cause. Sin must be brought to the foot of the cross.

I saw a rather amusing thread in the comment section of one of our YouTube video witnessing encounters. It went like this:

First person: "Ray gets rather combative sometimes. You catch more flies with honey than with vinegar."

Second person: "I've heard him say, 'That is true. If you are catching flies.'"

First person: "I stand corrected."

Despite his standing corrected, let's look at the first person's original thought for a moment. The *honey* referred to could be either a loving attitude or the sweetness of the gospel. If it's a loving attitude and people are heading for hell, love would warn, plead, and even be combative in the hope that they would turn from their sins. True love will always be passionate in such a situation.

If the honey is the sweetness of the gospel, the Bible says that the preaching of the cross is foolishness to the unsaved. Sinners not only think the gospel is irrelevant foolishness but also love the darkness of sin more than the light of the gospel. In other words, sin is sweeter to them than the gospel. Therefore, the loving thing to do is to show them the danger they are in—because they are not going to forsake their darling pleasures of sin easily. Remember, Scripture says that by the fear of the Lord, people depart from evil. And for sinners to fear God, they need to hear God's law and understand that they are under its wrath. This will make the gospel sweet.

The reality is that everyone will be held accountable before God, whether or not they have understood the gospel. The standard will be the moral law. While God reveals Himself to all of us, He has still given us the responsibility of preaching His word. The current objection should be more challenging to believers than to anyone else.

STUDY QUESTIONS

1. What do the heavens do in reference to God's glory (see Ps. 19:1)?
2. Explain why a judge is under no obligation to give a criminal anything but justice.
3. Why do Christians have an obligation to the lost?
4. In which Bible verse does Paul speak of being in debt to the lost?
5. How often do you think deeply of the fate of the unsaved?
6. Can you think of ways to overcome apathy when it comes to evangelism?
7. Why is it a mistake to offer the gospel as the cure for alcoholism or drug addiction?

17. "Why does God allow evil?"

Sue and I became tired of watching television news every night. There was nothing but stories of war, violence, rape, and murder. So we read the Bible instead. In the Bible, we read stories of war, violence, rape, and murder. It seems that we can no more get away from evil than a fish can get away from water. People who ask our current question have probably also noticed the evil all around them.

Let's imagine that you don't like the prevalence of evil in our society, and you decide to create your own utopia by moving to an island far away from modern-day corruption. You choose a group of secular people who are the cream of society and go there. You take the initiative and draft twelve precautionary laws in case someone does do something wrong in this new world. You propose that the following be unlawful: murder, rape, theft, lying, stealing, adultery, fornication, same-sex unions, blasphemy, extortion, abortion, and pedophilia.

But there's a problem. Your society doesn't like the rules. These cream-of-the-crop people say that adultery, abortion, same-sex relationships, and fornication are not evil. Most of them also say that lying and blasphemy are just a part of life and that to call such things "evil" is ridiculous. When you set up a forum to discuss these issues, there is immediate anger toward you for your intolerance. A number of them call for you to be arrested for hate speech. Your utopia breaks down before it even starts because of the secular world's definition of what is good and evil.

When someone asks why God allows evil, it's essential to define what they mean by *evil*. Are they confining evil to Nazi Germany, the Mafia, mass murder, and the atrocities of war? And what do they suggest God should do to those who are evil? Are they saying there should be a place of punishment? As we have seen, there must be societal retribution for evil acts, or those who govern become evil themselves. If a man commits murder or rape and is not punished by society, that society is complicit and therefore corrupt.

By calling for God to punish evil, the world paints itself into a tight corner. This happens because, whether they realize it, God is perfectly good and therefore must punish all evil. When the apostle Paul stood up in Athens and preached the gospel, he said that God had appointed a day in which He would judge the world in righteousness (see Acts 17:30–31). But Paul added something wonderful. He said that God "winked" (v. 30 KJV) at his hearers' "times of ignorance." In other words, the kindly judge overlooked the evil humanity had done, because He is rich in mercy. He delayed sentencing so that the criminal could think about his crimes and reconsider his plea.

When it comes to evil, the world wants to have its cake and eat it too. It was known for years that Hollywood had sexual predators, but in 2017 the dam burst. What was once conveniently hidden in the darkness of the entertainment and media industry suddenly came to light.

How common is sexual misconduct in Hollywood? The first number you see is 94%—and your eyes pop with incredulity.

But it's true: Almost *every one* of hundreds of women questioned in an exclusive survey by USA TODAY say they have experienced some form of sexual harassment or assault during their careers in Hollywood.[1]

Sexual abuse, like STDs, is one of the negative consequences in a society that has thrown off moral restraint. If anything goes, then there are no real boundaries. What society doesn't consider, however, is that we have to live with the negative consequences of our "freedom."

Take, for example, a certain popular television network that hires foxy ladies to host its programs. They are almost always attractive blondes who wear revealing fitted dresses and have long, shapely legs that are often filmed from a low angle. This is a form of sexual exploitation, but few complain because the women are highly paid and the male viewership is through the roof. But there's a negative consequence. The network's own sexual predators couldn't keep their hands off the merchandise, resulting in dismissals and millions of dollars being paid out in hush money.[2]

The legal definition of *sexual predator* varies from state to state, but law enforcement usually uses the term when referring to someone who searches for victims. This is regardless of whether the predator actually commits a crime. Civil law would consider someone a sexual predator if they are peering through a gap in the curtains of a bedroom window, hoping to see people undressing or engaging in sexual activity. But there are other sexual predators the law ignores. There are millions who regularly peer through a window of a television or movie screen at people highly paid to undress and have sex. These actors prostitute themselves for the world's entertainment.

If the world wants to weed out the evil of sexual predators, they should examine their own evil hearts first. Listen to what the Bible says about those who restrict their judgments to others: "Therefore you are inexcusable, O man, whoever you are who judge, for in whatever you judge another you condemn yourself; for you who judge practice the same things" (Rom. 2:1).

Hollywood has always pushed the envelope when it comes to sexual entertainment. The dam that held back the polluted waters for more than twenty years was the Hays Code.

> The Motion Picture Production Code was the set of industry moral guidelines that was applied to most United States motion pictures released by major studios from 1930 to 1968. It is also popularly known as the Hays Code, after Will H. Hays, who was the president of the Motion Picture Producers and Distributors of America (MPPDA) from 1922 to 1945. Under Hays' leadership, the MPPDA, later known as the Motion Picture Association of America (MPAA), adopted the Production Code in 1930 and began rigidly enforcing it in mid-1934. The Production Code spelled out what was acceptable and what was unacceptable content for motion pictures produced for a public audience in the United States.[3]

In the 1950s when the code was dropped, cracks began appearing in the dam, and it burst via the sexual revolution of the 1960s. Since then, the world has been flooded with the belief that there are no moral boundaries except one. All sex is morally acceptable but with one condition—consent. If there isn't a nod of consent, then an individual is deemed a sexual predator. But evil becomes good if the party is complicit.

There is a well-known incident in Scripture in which a couple was caught having illicit sex. The man was let off the hook, and the woman was dragged alone into the public square and accused of sexual misconduct. Religious leaders called for her blood to be shed. They wanted evil to be judged. But Jesus famously said, "He who is without sin among you, let him throw a stone at her first" (John 8:7).

The reason that God isn't immediately punishing evil is because the ones who call for wrath are standing in His line of fire. He is not willing that any perish but that all come to repentance. So before we implore the judge to bring His wrath down on evil men and women, we had better move out from under the gavel.

STUDY QUESTIONS

1. Why do you think the Bible is filled with so many incidents of evil?
2. Why isn't it possible to create a society that is free from sin?
3. What is the reason society paints itself into a tight corner when it calls on God to punish evil?
4. Why did God "wink" at the ignorance of Paul's hearers in Athens?

Ray Comfort

5. What are some of the negative consequences for a world that has no moral boundaries?
6. What Bible verse condemns those who judge others and do the same things?
7. Why doesn't God immediately punish evil?

18. "What's so bad about other religions?"

For the last forty years I've been gathering material for a book titled *101 Good Things about Growing Old*. So far I have one: you get to watch old movies again for the first time. Despite the promise that old age is our "golden" years, there's nothing gold about old. It's when we're welcomed into the world of heartburn, hair loss, hernias, back pain, joint pain, foot pain, kidney stones, gallstones, stomach ulcers, insomnia, memory loss, hearing loss, vision loss, muscle loss, yellow teeth, canker sores, age spots, wrinkled skin, bags under the eyes, sties in the eyes, and bouncing floaters. But then things get seriously bad.

In the early 1950s, the song "You Will Never Grow Old" became popular. The chorus goes as follows:

> You will never grow old
> While there's love in your heart.
> Time may silver your golden hair
> As you dream in an old rocking-chair.[1]

The sentiment was sweet, but in real life, it was sour. The singer, Nat King Cole, died at the young age of forty-five. Even the person the song was about grew old and died. If we

don't die young, life becomes a battle to keep our health—
a battle that no matter how courageously we fight, we all
will lose.

That's life, and it's unspeakably depressing—if you are unsaved. As Christians, we do reluctantly grow old and die but
with the glorious knowledge that even though outwardly we
are perishing, inwardly we are getting better: "Therefore we
do not lose heart. Though outwardly we are wasting away, yet
inwardly we are being renewed day by day" (2 Cor. 4:16 NIV).

Until I became a Christian, it never dawned on me to wonder why billions of people from every nation are interested
in God. Now I know it's because we will all die. God will
not die, and our only hope as dying creatures is to somehow
get to Him. Death is an impassable dark wall with only one
small door that has "God" written on it, and that promises
some light.

Because of the depressing reality of life and impending
death, billions seek comfort through religion, hoping that
God will open that door if they strive to live a good life. But
no prayer, no self-denial, no financial gift or religious work
will turn God from His pursuit of justice. It's sometimes
difficult to understand why so many are deceived by false
hope. But there is a reason for it: "This I say, therefore, and
testify in the Lord, that you should no longer walk as the
rest of the Gentiles walk, in the futility of their mind, having
their understanding darkened, being alienated from the life
of God, because of the ignorance that is in them, because
of the blindness of their heart" (Eph. 4:17–18).

The understanding of the lost has been darkened. They
need the light of the law to show them that they cannot save
themselves. The great divide between mercy and works is

seen in the story Jesus told about two men who went to the temple to pray:

> He spoke this parable to some who trusted in themselves that they were righteous, and despised others: "Two men went up to the temple to pray, one a Pharisee and the other a tax collector. The Pharisee stood and prayed thus with himself, 'God, I thank You that I am not like other men—extortioners, unjust, adulterers, or even as this tax collector. I fast twice a week; I give tithes of all that I possess.' And the tax collector, standing afar off, would not so much as raise his eyes to heaven, but beat his breast, saying, 'God, be merciful to me a sinner!' I tell you, this man went down to his house justified rather than the other; for everyone who exalts himself will be humbled, and he who humbles himself will be exalted." (Luke 18:9–14)

The tax collector threw himself upon the mercy of the judge. He was justified, because he let go of his own efforts to save himself and trusted in mercy alone.

Religions such as Hinduism, Islam, Buddhism, and others are made up of billions of people who are wondering what happens to them when they die. And they need God's mercy just as much as we do.

Posing with Parrots

Each week, people show up at Huntington Beach (where I regularly preach in the open air), and they often say they appreciate our television program. Late in 2017, a couple from Wisconsin asked if they could take a quick picture with me. I told them that I would be honored and looked for someone to take our photo. The only person who wasn't busy was a gentleman who had been coming to the beach each Saturday for about two months. He made his money by placing his two large and colorful parrots on tourists' shoulders, and they would take pictures of their spouse or child posing with the birds and tip him.

I asked, "There's a couple here from Wisconsin who would like a photo. Could you possibly take it?" It would only take a few seconds, and then he could get back to his business.

He kindly came over, but instead of taking a quick picture of the three of us, he had me stand next to the woman. Then he put a parrot on her shoulder (she was clearly uncomfortable). Then he firmly pulled me next to her, put a parrot on my arm, and had her husband take our picture. Then it was the husband's turn to be pushed and pulled, parroted and posed for the perfect picture.

The miscommunication was understandable. I wanted him to take a picture of us, but he thought I wanted him to take a picture of us with parrots, because that's what he did all day. I whispered an apology to the couple and slipped the man a tip.

When we say something to the ungodly, they hear it as something else. We say, "Get right with God, and He will give you the gift of everlasting life!" But they hear, "Get religious. Give up those false religions and the pleasure they give you, and in return you will be rewarded with Heaven." Their understanding has been darkened. We, therefore, have to be very clear with our words. My parrot miscommunication cost me a few dollars, but a miscommunication of the gospel due to bad theology could cost far more. That's why we need to continually pull back and ask, "Am I evangelizing biblically? Am I doing what Jesus did? Am I communicating by using the moral law to bring the knowledge of sin and, thus, preparing the heart for grace? Or am I for some reason merely speaking to the intellect and avoiding the conscience?" If their understanding remains darkened, they won't repent and trust the Savior. They will simply make a religious decision to make some changes and then sit in darkness among God's people.

The Tearless Eye

We must not only examine *what* we speak but also *how* we speak to the unsaved. Are we motivated by a love for the lost, or do we just love apologetics? Charles Spurgeon said, "I am certain that to preach the wrath of God with a hard heart, cold lip, tearless eyes, and an unfeeling spirit is to harden men—not to benefit them."[2]

People who ask about other religions also need to hear God's law. Their question shows they don't understand the motivation of the religious. Therefore, use the answer to give them light on their condition as well as that of the religious.

One of the most offensive biblical doctrines to the world is that Jesus is the only way to God. We can't deny it. He is the one who said, "I am the way, the truth, and the life. No one comes to the Father except through me" (John 14:6). But there is a way to present this great truth inoffensively and without compromise.

When we speak of other religions, we must do so with respect. We don't want to say they are deceived or wrong, and we don't want to have a condescending or self-righteous tone. I do this by adding the word *great* when referring to them. They are great in size rather than in doctrine. I say that all the great religions, such as Islam, Hinduism, and Buddhism, have one thing in common. They are what is known as "works righteousness" religions. This means they teach that one must *do* something to make it to Heaven—to attain everlasting life. People must fast, pray, repent, lie on a bed of nails, sit on hard pews, do good works, face Mecca, and so on. These things are done in the hope that their actions will even the scales with God. These people are trusting that their good will outweigh their bad.

But when the moral law makes its entrance, it reveals that God is a perfect judge and that we are desperately wicked criminals who have broken the law a multitude of times. This truth radically changes the dynamic. It shows us that what we are offering the judge is not "good works" to balance the scales but despicable attempts to bribe the judge of the universe. God will not be paid off. He will not be bribed to turn a blind eye to evil. Trying to bribe an earthly judge will get you into big trouble. How much more will it anger God!

Proverbs 15:8 says, "The sacrifice of the wicked is an abomination to the Lord." No amount of sacrifice (or payment) on our part can cause God to turn away from our transgressions. His holiness demands retribution:

> Those who trust in their wealth
> And boast in the multitude of their riches,
> None of them can by any means redeem [another],
> Nor give to God a ransom for [them]—
> For the redemption of their souls is costly.
> (Ps. 49:6–8)

But God is rich in mercy. He provided the payment Himself, in Christ. He provided the sacrificial Lamb whose suffering satisfied the demands of eternal justice. We broke the law and Jesus paid the fine, evidenced in His dying words, "It is finished!" In other words, "The debt has been paid!" That means that our case can be legally dismissed. We can walk out of the courtroom, our death sentence having been commuted. We can live forever!

This wonderful gospel is universal. It is good news for Hindus, Muslims, Buddhists, atheists, and agnostics, as well as religious people who think they can live a good life, please God, and make it to Heaven.

STUDY QUESTIONS

1. How is it that those in Christ can grow old gracefully?
2. Why do you think so many are involved in some form of religion?
3. What is the great deception of religion?
4. Why is the hope of many in vain?
5. According to Ephesians 4:17–18, what is the state of mind of the ungodly?
6. In Luke 18:9–14, how was the tax collector justified?
7. By what should the Christian be motivated to evangelize?

19. "Seeing is believing. Why do I need faith? Faith is for weak people."

Years ago, someone sent me a video produced by well-known atheist and magician Penn Jillette (of Penn and Teller fame) in which he expressed a frustrating intellectual quandary. He marveled that anyone could believe the foolish stories in the book of Genesis. In particular, he was astonished that intelligent people, some of whom he was friends with, embraced the silly story of Noah's ark and the flood.

I watched a few other videos made by him, and it was evident that he hated the very thought of God. It is said that he is so staunch in his beliefs, he crosses out "In God We Trust" from every dollar bill that comes his way. He even went to the trouble of making other videos about the Scriptures. In one, he twisted a verse to say something it didn't and then showed his disdain by kicking a copy of the Bible and throwing other copies over his shoulder. He had questions, but it was evident he wasn't seeking answers. And so this popular despiser of Christianity was left marveling as to why intelligent people believed the stories in the book of Genesis.

The marveling of "despisers" is addressed in Scripture. When Paul preached the gospel in Antioch, he said:

Beware . . . lest what has been spoken in the prophets come upon you:

> "Behold, you despisers,
> Marvel and perish!
> For I work a work in your days,
> A work which you will by no means believe,
> Though one were to declare it to you."
> (Acts 13:40–41)

Notice that this passage says marveling despisers will "by no means believe" the "work" that God will do, even if it is declared to them. Proud people who ask questions like the one currently being considered are often offended by the word *believe*. They believe that faith is intellectually beneath them, even though all healthy human relationships, all business transactions, and all political dealings between parties and nations rest on the foundation of faith. If there's no trust, there is no relationship. If I don't have faith in you and believe what you say, it indicates that I think you are a liar.

The "work" of God verse 41 refers to is that He chose "the foolish things of the world to confound the wise" (1 Cor. 1:27 KJV). He deliberately put incidents into His Word that confound the worldly wise because they are an offense to the proud mind. Who in his right mind would ever believe that Noah literally built an ark and that all those animals came in two by two? Anyone with any intellectual dignity would never stoop to believe such childish foolishness. But such is the manifold wisdom of God; He has chosen foolish things to confound the worldly wise.

Jesus warned that we must stoop to enter the kingdom of God. To be saved from death and hell, we must become as little children and simply believe the gospel, offensive though that may be to the human ego. As in Noah's day, those today who do not believe are shut out of the kingdom of God. Those who refuse to believe will be left marveling and will perish in their sins.

The irony is that the book of Genesis is a gold mine for intellectual scrutiny. If anyone with a humble heart studies the case for the Noahic flood, they will find great evidence for its credibility. The proud attack Genesis with an army of straw men. If one argument crumbles, they have a battalion of others lined up for battle. They continue the fight, because, like Mr. Jillette, they aren't seeking the truth. They are simply trying to justify their own love for sin.

When I fish for men, I'm looking for those who are humble. I test the waters with three questions: first, "Do you think there's an afterlife?"; second, "Do you think you're a good person?"; and third, "Are you afraid of dying?" The way they answer these questions lets me know if they are humble or proud. And then I cut my cloth to fit. God resists the proud and gives grace to the humble, and we should do the same.

The proud get God's law, and the humble get the gospel. I often find that the law will give the proud a reason to become one of the humble. The humble are the ones who will listen to how Genesis uniquely addresses the big questions about our origins, our purpose, the reality of evil, human suffering, disease, the reason for death, and even the promise of life that is found in Jesus Christ alone.

People who ask our current question are proud. They don't think they need to place their faith in anything. The only thing that will humble them is the reality of Jesus.

Ray Comfort

1. Why does faith offend a proud person?
2. Name some ways in which we exercise faith.
3. What is the implication when we refuse to trust someone?
4. What has God chosen to confound the wise?
5. What are three effective questions to ask someone to learn if they are humble of heart?
6. Who should be given the law and why?
7. Who should be given the gospel and why?

20. "I can murder a hundred people, then give my heart to Jesus and go to Heaven?"

I'm not a big fan of the modern plea bargain that is so often used in our court system. A plea bargain is any agreement in a criminal case between the prosecutor and defendant in which the defendant agrees to plead guilty to a particular charge in return for some concession from the prosecutor. For example, a murderer may escape the death penalty and get life in prison if he shows authorities where he buried the dismembered body of his victim.

In speaking of the difference between the modern plea bargain and genuine forgiveness, University of Pennsylvania Law School professor Stephanos Bibas said, "Modern American criminal justice . . . has little room for forgiveness. It has become an assembly line, a plea-bargaining factory that speeds up cases and reduces costs by sacrificing the offender's and victim's day in court."[1]

The essential difference between the plea bargain and the forgiveness we have in Christ is the presence of contrition in the believer. Contrition is a genuine sorrow for sin. While this has nothing to do with earning God's mercy, the Scriptures tell us that it is the pathway to genuine repentance: "For godly sorrow produces repentance leading to salvation, not to be regretted; but the sorrow of the world produces death" (2 Cor. 7:10).

The gospel we preach should never be "plead guilty to sin and God will change your sentence from hell to Heaven." That is a bargain indeed, but such a message has the danger of producing false converts. It circumnavigates the process of contrition. A heinous criminal may avail himself of the modern plea bargain and yet have no sorrow for his crime. This cannot happen in Christ, and we must never cheapen the gospel and cheat our hearers by offering it.

When Nathan preached to David after he sinned with Bathsheba, he said, "Why have you despised the commandment of the LORD?" (2 Sam. 12:9). The king had sinned against God through his adultery and murder , and we see his heartfelt contrition in his prayer in Psalm 51:

> Have mercy upon me, O God,
> According to Your lovingkindness;
> According to the multitude of Your tender mercies,
> Blot out my transgressions.
> Wash me thoroughly from my iniquity,
> And cleanse me from my sin.
> For I acknowledge my transgressions,
> And my sin is always before me.
> Against You, You only, have I sinned,
> And done this evil in Your sight—
> That You may be found just when You speak,
> And blameless when You judge. (vv. 1–4)

Professor Bibas further stated, "Centuries ago, contrition and forgiveness rituals were central to colonial criminal justice, and there is good reason to bring back this emphasis today."[2] Bibas cites *Crime and Punishment in American History* by Lawrence Friedman, which described the colonial trial as "an occasion for repentance and reintegration: a ritual for reclaiming lost sheep and restoring them to the flock" and noted the colonial expectation that defendants awaiting execution would be penitent and confess and that, when defendants threw themselves on the court's mercy, courts might be "patient and lenient."[3]

The difference in colonial days was that the merciful plea bargain was closely aligned with the forgiveness we have in Christ. Plus, crime was not as prevalent as it is today. Now criminals are treated like customers at an efficient supermarket. Hopefully, a prosecutor has some desire to see a criminal's contrition. He may show photos of the victim in the hope that the defendant's conscience comes alive when he realizes the suffering he caused to the victim and their family.

It should be our hope also that when the gospel is preached, sinners come to understand the terrible suffering they caused to the innocent victim of their crimes. That suffering is evidenced in the cross of Jesus Christ. This is why we must preach the moral law to show our guilt, future punishment to show our fate, and the innocent Lamb to show the terrible cost. All this is to reveal the sweet sound of amazing grace.

Once again, take care when answering someone who asks the question "I can murder a hundred people, then give my heart to Jesus and go to Heaven?" It's an exaggeration to show that mercy is unreasonable. But they are right. The word *unreasonable* is defined as "beyond the limits of acceptability or fairness." It's not fair that God should extend mercy to a murderer or a rapist. It's not fair that He should be merciful to an adulterer, a fornicator, and terrible sinners like you and me. But His mercy is offered to all guilty sinners, who once they have seen the cross will thank God that He is rich in mercy. There's a reason Psalm 136 begins with "Oh, give thanks to the Lord, for He is good! For His mercy endures forever" (v. 1) and repeats "for His mercy endures forever" another twenty-five times.

Can a murderer be forgiven? Of course. We see that with King David and the apostle Paul. If it's sickening to us that God would forgive someone who has taken the life of another human being, we had better keep that disgust to ourselves. It may be rooted in empathy for the murdered victim, but God forgives whom He will. It is His prerogative, not ours.

Atheists will sometimes drop Hitler's name into the question: "So if Hitler believed at the last moment, he made it to Heaven, but the Jews he murdered went to hell?" The answer to that question is a categorical no. We know that the Bible says that demons "believe" and tremble (see James 2:19). The Bible says that salvation is a free gift of God (see Rom. 6:23). We are saved by grace and grace alone (see Eph. 2:8–9). No one can earn salvation by repenting or even by believing. It is grace that saves us, and the way to partake of that grace is by God-granted repentance (see 2 Tim. 2:24–26) and faith alone in Jesus.

If Hitler "believed" at the last minute, it wouldn't mean that he made it to Heaven. It is true that there are numerous verses that speak of the promise of salvation with no mention of repentance. These merely say to believe on Jesus Christ and you will be saved (see Acts 16:31; Rom. 10:9). However, the Bible makes it clear that God is holy and human beings are sinful, and that sin separates the two (see Isa. 59:1–2).

Without repentance from sin, wicked men cannot have fellowship with a holy God. We are dead in our trespasses and sins (see Eph. 2:1), and until we forsake them through God-given repentance, we cannot be made alive in Christ. The Scriptures speak of "repentance unto life" (Acts 11:18 KJV). We turn from sin to the Savior. This is why Paul preached "repentance toward God, and faith toward our Lord Jesus Christ" (Acts 20:21).

The first public word Jesus preached was "repent" (Matt. 4:17). John the Baptist began his ministry the same way (see Matt. 3:2). Jesus told His hearers that without repentance, they would perish (see Luke 13:3). If belief is all that is necessary for salvation, then the logical conclusion is that one need never repent.

However, the Bible tells us that false converts "believe" and yet are not saved (see Luke 8:13); they remain "workers of iniquity" (Luke 13:27 KJV). Look at the warning of Scripture: "If we say that we have fellowship with Him, and walk in darkness, we lie and do not practice the truth" (1 John 1:6).

Scripture also says, "Whoever conceals their sins does not prosper, but the one who confesses and renounces them finds mercy" (Prov. 28:13). Jesus said that there was joy in Heaven over one sinner who "repents" (Luke 15:10). If there is no repentance, there is no joy, because there is no salvation.

When Peter preached on the Day of Pentecost, he commanded his hearers to repent "for the remission of sins" (Acts 2:38). Without repentance, there is no remission of sins; we are still under God's wrath. Peter further said, "Repent . . . and be converted, that your sins may be blotted out" (Acts 3:19). We cannot be converted unless we repent. God Himself "commands all people everywhere"—which leaves no exceptions—"to repent" (Acts 17:30 NIV). Peter said a similar thing at Pentecost: "Repent, and be baptized every one of you" (Acts 2:38 KJV).

If repentance wasn't necessary for salvation, why then did Jesus command that repentance be preached to all nations (see Luke 24:47)? With so many Scriptures speaking of the necessity of repentance for salvation, one can only suspect that those who preach salvation without repentance are strangers to repentance themselves and thus strangers to true conversion.

While it is possible that if someone like Hitler repented and trusted in Jesus alone, he could be saved, I would always defer the question to the fact that it is God's right to save whom He will. Then go back to the question of the questioner's salvation. That's what should truly concern them.

STUDY QUESTIONS

1. What's the difference between a modern-day plea bargain and the forgiveness we have in Christ?
2. Define *contrition*.
3. Where did Jesus mention repentance?
4. What is the danger of circumnavigating the process of contrition?
5. Highlight evidence of David's sorrow for his sin in Psalm 51:1–4.
6. How do we best show grace to be amazing?
7. Whose prerogative is it to forgive?

Conclusion

I want to give you some encouragement as you head out into the world of sharing the gospel.

Let me tell you one more story. Occasionally, I think of the Bible verse about every man sitting under his own vine (see Mic. 4:4). It speaks of contentment. This was one of those sitting-under-the-vine moments. I had fried a fresh egg for lunch, hadn't burned the toast, and had a glass of cool milk and a freshly baked cupcake. I felt overwhelmed with contentment and gratitude to God for such a moment. I placed the plate, which included my glass of milk and a saltshaker, on the arm of my La-Z-Boy recliner and switched on the TV to watch some news.

A memory came to mind—a memory of my family at a restaurant. The waitress had just arrived at our table with our food, and I had naively taken a glass of milk off her full tray. I was just trying to be helpful, but what I did sent her and everyone around our table into a panic. I had no idea that the milk was her "balance" for the rest of the food on the tray. You can guess what happened next. It was a good life lesson for the wise of heart.

Back to my moment of contentment. I sat down in my recliner, then picked up the saltshaker off the plate. I yelled, "Oh no!" as gravity moved the milk from the plate to the floor three feet down. The salt was the plate's balance! I should have known. And the fall wasn't just downward; it was down and across onto our carpet and sheepskin rug. As I looked at the disaster area, I thought of Sue. The only one that looked happy was my dog. This was an answer to his prayers. I mumbled a resigned "Go for it!" This was his awaited promised land, and he rushed face-first into the mess.

If things don't go right for you during a witnessing encounter, mop up the best you can, learn from what happened, and determine to do better next time. Make sure there is a next time. I didn't stop drinking milk just because of a spill.

Having the Contrast

Young people are often criticized for overuse of cell phones. I can't fault them for a moment, because I do the same. I love modern technology. I love my iPhone, iPad, iPod, PC, and laptop. This is because I remember tapping out entire books on a typewriter. I remember having to get up and change a TV channel because there was no such thing as a remote control. I remember having to get out of my car to physically open a garage door, missing a phone call and never knowing who it was from, and waiting for two weeks for photos to be developed. I know what it's like to watch sports on a fourteen-inch black-and-white TV. Nowadays I watch high definition rugby on a sixty-inch flat screen. Having these comparisons from my youth gives me a huge advantage over today's generation. I'm in awe every time I use a remote, my phone, my iPad, or my TV. I have a sense of appreciation and gratitude that young people don't have.

So it is with my Christian walk. I was once lost and so appreciate being found. I was once without hope and purpose; in Christ I now have both. I was once held captive by death, and there isn't a moment of time I'm not bursting with gratitude that I have everlasting life in Christ. It is this gratitude toward God and concern for the unsaved that is the fuel that drives me to reach the lost.

More Final Motivation

For the many years I preached open air in the heart of my hometown of Christchurch, New Zealand, I had a way to encourage myself when the going got a little tough. When I was mocked for my faith or had a day when milk spilled, I would say, "I have the privilege of preaching the everlasting gospel, in the last days, in the uttermost part of the earth, in the city that bears the name of the Lord." And I didn't use the word *privilege* lightly. One of the most profound revelations I ever had was that God really didn't need me. In Luke 19:30–31, Jesus told His disciples, "Go into the village opposite you, where as you enter you will find a colt tied, on which no one has ever sat. Loose it and bring it here. And if anyone asks you, 'Why are you loosing it?' thus you shall say to him, 'Because the Lord has need of it.'"

The Creator of the universe had need of it. But He didn't really need it, because in a split second He could have created ten million donkeys. But Jesus needed it for a purpose.

God is in need of nothing and nobody. He doesn't need oxygen to breathe or light to see or food to live, and He doesn't need me to fulfill His eternal purposes. I remember the very moment I had this revelation. It was July 28, 1982, the day when the popular singer Keith Green died in a plane crash. It shocked me. It shocked me because God was using him in a wonderful way to encourage millions, and in a moment of time he was gone. My naive thought was, "Keith Green . . . dead! Lord, who have you got left?"

God didn't need Keith Green, wonderful though he was, and He doesn't need you or me. Yet He has conceded to use you and me to bring the message of eternal life to this world. The pauper is allowed to speak on behalf of the prince. The lowly donkey carries the King of Kings. Privileged indeed, beyond words.

Therefore, don't let anything stop you from appreciating this honor. Cast off fear, apathy, discouragement, busyness, and the subtlety of hidden pride. Fear only God, love the lost, cultivate a tender conscience, pray daily for wisdom, and let your little light shine. Be a John the Baptist, and with the help of God you can fill up the valleys, bring down the mountains, and prepare the way of the Lord so that lost sinners will one day see His glory.

Thank you for taking the time to read this book. I'm both humbled and encouraged that you did. We need people like you—faithful laborers who let love overcome their fears and think of others rather than themselves. Always keep in mind that it's normal for those who reach out to the lost to feel like a one-person wave at the Super Bowl. But you're never alone "for we are labourers together with God" (1 Cor. 3:9 KJV).

The combined accomplishments of great secular men and women in history don't hold a candle to being used by God to bring the light of salvation to one human soul. You are more important than Shakespeare, Newton, Gandhi, Florence Nightingale, and George Washington. Their legacy was temporal. Yours is eternal. Even your feet are beautiful: "How beautiful are the feet of those who preach the gospel of peace, who bring glad tidings of good things!" (Rom. 10:15).

Now get those beautiful feet moving!

Notes

Big Things First—Dealing with the Goliath of Fear

1. "Survey: Christians Are Not Spreading the Gospel," George Barna, November 30, 2017, http://www.georgebarna.com/research-flow/2017/11/30/survey-christians-are-not-spreading-the-gospel.
2. "We must not excuse ourselves, but force ourselves to the irksome task until it becomes easy." Charles H. Spurgeon, *Spurgeon Gold*, comp. Ray Comfort (Gainesville, FL: Bridge-Logos, 2005), 94.

More Important Than Apologetics

1. Charles H. Spurgeon, "All of Grace," Believer's Web, March 26, 2003, https://believersweb.org/view.cfm?ID=223.
2. To watch these videos for free, go to YouTube and search "Living Waters" (over sixty million views).

Chapter 1 "If God is supposed to be in control of the world, why does it seem so out of control?"

1. Donald G. McNeil Jr., "The Flu Outbreak Has Peaked but Still Has Weeks to Go," *New York Times*, updated February 26, 2018, https://www.nytimes.com/2018/01/18/health/flu-season-facts.html.

Chapter 2 "What sort of God would threaten to torture people in hell forever just because they don't believe in Him?" (Part One)

1. "Prison for 3 Northwest Pilots Who Flew Jet While Drunk," *New York Times*, October 27, 1990, http://www.nytimes.com/1990/10/27/us/prison-for-3-northwest-pilots-who-flew-jet-while-drunk.html.
2. Augustus Toplady, "Rock of Ages," 1763, public domain.
3. A. W. Tozer, *The Knowledge of the Holy* (New York: HarperCollins, 2009), 89.

Chapter 3 "What sort of God would threaten to torture people in hell forever just because they don't believe in Him?" (Part Two)

1. Cornell Law School, accessed November 2, 2018, https://www.law.cornell.edu/uscode/text/28/453. The Cornell website has other information about judges as well.

2. "Interesting Facts about Lady Justice: A Legal Symbol of American Justice!," interesting facts.tv, accessed November 2, 2018, https://interestingfacts.tv/amazing-facts/interesting-facts-about-lady-justice-a-legal-symbol-of-american-justice/.

3. "Americans Divided on the Importance of Church," Barna Group, March 24, 2014, https://www.barna.com/research/americans-divided-on-the-importance-of-church/. See the Barna website for many great resources for discussions with believers and unbelievers alike.

4. Ray Comfort, *God Has a Wonderful Plan for Your Life: The Myth of the Modern Message* (Bellflower, CA: Living Waters Publications, 2010), at Living Waters.com.

Chapter 4 "Why should I care about what happens after I die if you can't even prove that there's life after death?"

1. Alyssa Newcomb, "CES 2018: Power Outage at Tech's Biggest Trade Show," NBC News, updated January 10, 2018, https://www.nbcnews.com/tech/tech-news/ces-2018-power-outage-tech-s-biggest-trade-show-n836551.

2. C. H. Spurgeon, "Christ's Resurrection and Our Newness of Life" (March 29, 1891), Bible Bulletin Board, accessed November 2, 2018, http://www.biblebb.com/files/spurgeon/2197.htm.

3. I love this song. Gaither Vocal Band, "Because He Lives," by Bill Gaither, track 9 on *Alleluia! Praise Continues*, released August 8, 1993, Star Song Music. Read all the lyrics at https://www.lyricsmode.com/lyrics/b/bill_gaither/because_he_lives.html.

Chapter 5 "How can you believe that God is love when there is so much suffering in the world?"

1. "My Way," English lyrics by Paul Anka, 1967, released and popularized by Frank Sinatra in 1969. If you're curious about the full lyrics, see https://genius.com/Frank-Sinatra-my-way-lyrics.

Chapter 6 "Isn't the God of the Old Testament different from the God of the New Testament?"

1. Pandit Dasa, "The 33 Million Gods of Hinduism," HuffPost, updated October 6, 2012, https://www.huffingtonpost.com/gadadhara-pandit-dasa/the-33-million-demigods-o_b_1737207.html.

Chapter 7 "Would you sacrifice your child if God asked you to?"

1. R. Stickney, "Father Accused of Trying to Sacrifice His Son," NBC San Diego, updated April 30, 2012, https://www.nbcsandiego.com/news/local/Father-Sacrifice-Son-Mount-Hope-Cemetery-Arrest-149393265.html.

2. Sue Bohlin, "Oprah: America's Beloved False Teacher," *Engage* (blog), May 24, 2011, http://blogs.bible.org/engage/sue_bohlin/oprah_america's_beloved_false_teacher.

Chapter 8 "Aren't religions the cause of more wars and suffering than anything else in history?"

1. Rabbi Alan Lurie, "Is Religion the Cause of Most Wars?," HuffPost, updated June 10, 2012, https://www.huffingtonpost.com/rabbi-alan-lurie/is-religion-the-cause-of-_b_1400766.html.

2. Charles Phillips and Alan Axelrod, *Encyclopedia of Wars*, 3 vols. (New York: Facts on File, 2004). This encyclopedia clarified all kinds of things for me. See also Lurie, "Is Religion the Cause?"

3. Lurie, "Is Religion the Cause"; "World War I vs. World War II," Diffen, accessed November 2, 2018, https://www.diffen.com/difference/World_War_I_vs_World_War_II.

4. Quoted in "Doesn't Religion Cause Most of the Conflict in the World?," *The Guardian*, July 2013, https://www.theguardian.com/commentisfree/2013/jul/02/religion-wars-conflict.

5. "Jonestown," FBI, accessed November 2, 2018, https://www.fbi.gov/history/famous-cases/jonestown.

6. Sally H., "10 People Who Give Atheism a Bad Name," Listverse, June 5, 2010, http://listverse.com/2010/06/05/10-people-who-give-atheism-a-bad-name/.

7. "Citizen's Guide to U.S. Federal Law on Child Pornography," US Department of Justice, updated December 12, 2017, https://www.justice.gov/criminal-ceos/citizens-guide-us-federal-law-child-pornography.

Chapter 9 "If God is so loving, why won't Christians let gay people be themselves?"

1. Rosie West, "17 Things Jesus Christ Said about Homosexuality," PinkNews, April 16, 2017, http://www.pinknews.co.uk/2017/04/16/easter-17-things-jesus-christ-said-about-homosexuality/. This is an example of the sloppy scriptural understanding of our modern culture.

2. "Watch the Dramatic Moment a Woman Emerges from Muddy Floodwaters," National Geographic, March 17, 2017, https://video.nationalgeographic.com/video/news/170317-peru-flooding-woman-escapes-vin.

Chapter 10 "Are you saying that you are going to Heaven, but millions of sincere Muslims, Hindus, and Buddhists are going to hell because they don't believe as you do?"

1. Wikipedia, s.v. "agnostic atheism," last edited October 4, 2018, https://en.wikipedia.org/wiki/Agnostic_atheism. Try to riddle through the whole explanation Wikipedia provides.

2. *Merriam-Webster Unabridged*, s.v. "agnostic," updated September 6, 2018, https://www.merriam-webster.com/dictionary/agnostic.

Chapter 12 "Why should we believe the biblical account of creation when evolution, which is proven science, says something different?"

1. Jena E. Pincott, "The Real Purpose of Eyebrows," *Psychology Today*, July 4, 2011, https://www.psychologytoday.com/blog/love-sex-and-babies/201107/the-real-purpose-eyebrows.

2. Pincott, "Real Purpose of Eyebrows."

3. Marc Montgomery, "September 3, 1939, the Horror Begins; Loss of SS Athenia," September 3, 2014, http://www.rcinet.ca/en/2014/09/03/september-3-1939-the-maelstrom-begins-loss-of-ss-athenia/.

4. "Richard Dawkins: 'Immoral' Not to Abort If Foetus Has Down's Syndrome," *The Guardian*, August 21, 2014, https://www.theguardian.com/science/2014/aug/21/richard-dawkins-immoral-not-to-abort-a-downs-syndrome-foetus.

5. Richard Dawkins, Twitter post, March 3, 2018, 9:15 a.m., https://mobile.twitter.com/RichardDawkins/status/969939225180364805.

6. For a layperson's definition of *absolutism*, see Paige Montgomery, "History Midterm," accessed November 2, 2018, https://quizlet.com/19535763/history-midterm-flash-cards/.

Chapter 14 "You can't prove God exists; even if you could, if everything needs a cause, what god made God?"

1. Legal Dictionary, s.v. "proof," The Free Dictionary, accessed November 2, 2018, https://legal-dictionary.thefreedictionary.com/proof. There are other definitions at the same source.

2. Alok Jha, "What Is the Second Law of Thermodynamics?," *The Guardian*, December 1, 2013, https://www.theguardian.com/science/2013/dec/01/what-is-the-second-law-of-thermodynamics.

3. For these and more resources from Living Waters, see http://store.livingwaters.com/gospel-tracts/money.html.

4. Personal email, January 26, 2018.

Chapter 15 "Unbelievers are as good as any Christian, if not better, so why aren't we good enough to get into Heaven?"

1. Alex Mar, "Witches of America: How I Became Immersed in a Growing Movement," *The Guardian*, October 29, 2016, https://www.theguardian.com/life

andstyle/2016/oct/29/witches-of-america-alex-mar-pagan-witchcraft. This article is a good place to start if you want to know more about pagan worldviews.

Chapter 16 "What happens to those who have never heard the gospel?"

1. Charles H. Spurgeon, "The Immutability of God" (January 7, 1855), sec. 22, in *The Spurgeon Series 1855 & 1856: Unabridged Sermons in Modern Language*, ed. Larry and Marion Pierce (Green Forest, AR: Attic Books, 2012).

2. Wikipedia, s.v. "The Gates of Hell," accessed November 2, 2018, https://en.m.wikipedia.org/wiki/The_Gates_of_Hell. This article also has a picture of *The Thinker* if you've never seen it.

3. For these and more resources from Living Waters, see http://store.living waters.com/gospel-tracts/conversation-starters/ten-commandments-coin.html.

Chapter 17 "Why does God allow evil?"

1. Maria Puente and Cara Kelly, "How Common Is Sexual Misconduct in Hollywood?," *USA Today*, updated February 23, 2018, https://www.usatoday .com/story/life/people/2018/02/20/how-common-sexual-misconduct-hollywood /1083964001/, emphasis original.

2. Emily Shugerman, "Sexual Harassment Costs Fox News up to $110 Million in Last Nine Months," *Independent*, May 11, 2017, http://www.independent .co.uk/news/world/americas/fox-news-sexual-harassment-cases-payouts-settle ments-bill-o-reilly-roger-ailes-a7730556.html.

3. Wikipedia, s.v. "Motion Picture Production Code," accessed November 2, 2018, https://en.m.wikipedia.org/wiki/Motion_Picture_Production_Code.

Chapter 18 "What's so bad about other religions?"

1. Nat King Cole, vocalist, "You Will Never Grow Old," by Ruth Rand, released 1952, Capitol Records.

2. Charles H. Spurgeon, "Spurgeon's Sermons, Vol. 33: 1887," Christian Classics Ethereal Library, accessed October 30, 2018, https://www.ccel.org/ccel/spur geon/sermons33.lxii.html?highlight=to,preach,the,wrath,of,god,with,a,hard ,heart,and,cold,lip,tearless,eye#highlight.

Chapter 20 "I can murder a hundred people, then give my heart to Jesus and go to Heaven?"

1. Stephanos Bibas, "Forgiveness in Criminal Procedure" (2007), Faculty Scholarship, Paper 920, p. 329, https://scholarship.law.upenn.edu/faculty_scholarship/920.

2. Bibas, "Forgiveness in Criminal Procedure," 348.

3. Lawrence Friedman, *Crime and Punishment in American History* (New York: Basic Books, 1993), 25–26, quoted in Bibas, "Forgiveness in Criminal Procedure," 348n75.

Ray Comfort is the founder and CEO of Living Waters and the bestselling author of more than ninety books, including *God Has a Wonderful Plan for Your Life*, *How to Know God Exists*, and *The Evidence Bible*. He cohosts the award-winning television program *Way of the Master*, airing in almost two hundred countries, and is the executive producer of *180*, *Evolution vs. God*, *Audacity*, and other films. His ministry's YouTube channel has more than fifty-five million views. He is married to Sue and has three grown children.

STEPS TO PEACE WITH GOD

1. GOD'S PURPOSE: PEACE AND LIFE

God loves you and wants you to experience peace and life—abundant and eternal.

THE BIBLE SAYS ...

"We have peace with God through our Lord Jesus Christ." *Romans 5:1, NKJV*

"For God so loved the world that He gave His only begotten Son, that whoever believes in Him should not perish but have everlasting life." *John 3:16, NKJV*

"I have come that they may have life, and that they may have it more abundantly." *John 10:10, NKJV*

Since God planned for us to have peace and the abundant life right now, why are most people not having this experience?

2. OUR PROBLEM: SEPARATION FROM GOD

God created us in His own image to have an abundant life. He did not make us as robots to automatically love and obey Him, but gave us a will and a freedom of choice.

We chose to disobey God and go our own willful way. We still make this choice today. This results in separation from God.

THE BIBLE SAYS ...

"For all have sinned and fall short of the glory of God." *Romans 3:23, NKJV*

"For the wages of sin is death, but the gift of God is eternal life in Christ Jesus our Lord." *Romans 6:23, NKJV*

Our choice results in separation from God.

People (Sinful)   God (Holy)

Our Attempts

Through the ages, individuals have tried in many ways to bridge this gap ... without success ...

The Bible Says ...

"There is a way that seems right to a man, but its end is the way of death."
Proverbs 14:12, NKJV

"But your iniquities have separated you from your God; and your sins have hidden His face from you, so that He will not hear."
Isaiah 59:2, NKJV

There is only one remedy for this problem of separation.

3. God's Remedy: The Cross

Jesus Christ is the only answer to this problem. He died on the cross and rose from the grave, paying the penalty for our sin and bridging the gap between God and people.

The Bible Says ...

"For there is one God and one Mediator between God and men, the Man Christ Jesus."
1 Timothy 2:5, NKJV

"For Christ also suffered once for sins, the just for the unjust, that He might bring us to God."
1 Peter 3:18, NKJV

"But God shows his love for us in that while we were still sinners, Christ died for us." *Romans 5:8, ESV*

God has provided the only way ... we must make the choice ...

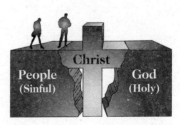

4. Our Response: Receive Christ

We must trust Jesus Christ and receive Him by personal invitation.

The Bible says ...

"Behold, I stand at the door and knock. If anyone hears My voice and opens the door, I will come in to him and dine with him, and he with Me." *Revelation 3:20, NKJV*

"But to all who did receive him, who believed in his name, he gave the right to become children of God." *John 1:12, ESV*

"If you confess with your mouth that Jesus is Lord and believe in your heart that God raised him from the dead, you will be saved." *Romans 10:9, ESV*

Are you here ... or here?

Is there any good reason why you cannot receive Jesus Christ right now?

How to Receive Christ:

1. Admit your need (say, "I am a sinner").
2. Be willing to turn from your sins (repent) and ask for God's forgiveness.
3. Believe that Jesus Christ died for you on the cross and rose from the grave.
4. Through prayer, invite Jesus Christ to come in and control your life through the Holy Spirit (receive Jesus as Lord and Savior).

What to Pray:

Dear God,
    I know that I am a sinner. I want to turn from my sins, and I ask for Your forgiveness. I believe that Jesus Christ is Your Son. I believe He died for my sins and that You raised Him to life. I want Him to come into my heart and to take control of my life. I want to trust Jesus as my Savior and follow Him as my Lord from this day forward.

                    In Jesus' Name, amen.

_____   _____
Date   Signature

God's Assurance: His Word

If you prayed this prayer,

the Bible says ...
"For 'everyone who calls on the name of the Lord will be saved.'"
Romans 10:13, ESV

Did you sincerely ask Jesus Christ to come into your life?
Where is He right now? What has He given you?

"For by grace you have been saved through faith. And this is not your
own doing; it is the gift of God, not a result of works, so that no one may
boast." *Ephesians 2:8–9, ESV*

the Bible says ...
"He who has the Son has life; he who does not have the Son of God does
not have life. These things I have written to you who believe in the name of
the Son of God, that you may know that you have eternal life, and that you
may continue to believe in the name of the Son of God."
1 John 5:12–13, NKJV

Receiving Christ, we are born into God's family through the
supernatural work of the Holy Spirit, who indwells every believer.
This is called regeneration or the "new birth."

This is just the beginning of a wonderful new life in Christ. To deepen
this relationship you should:

1. Read your Bible every day to know Christ better.
2. Talk to God in prayer every day.
3. Tell others about Christ.
4. Worship, fellowship, and serve with other Christians in a church where
   Christ is preached.
5. As Christ's representative in a needy world, demonstrate your new life by
   your love and concern for others.

God bless you as you do.

Franklin Graham

If you want further help in the decision you have made, write to:
Billy Graham Evangelistic Association
1 Billy Graham Parkway, Charlotte, NC 28201-0001

1-877-2GRAHAM (1-877-247-2426)
BillyGraham.org/commitment